THE GUIDE TO
CHINESE
HOROSCOPES

GERRY MAGUIRE THOMPSON
CONSULTANT: SHUEN-LIAN HSAIO

THE GUIDE TO CHINESE HOROSCOPES

- The Twelve Animal Signs • Personality and Aptitude
- Relationships and Compatibility • Work, Money and Health
- Horoscopes over Time

METRO BOOKS
New York

METRO BOOKS
New York

An Imprint of Sterling Publishing
387 Park Avenue South
New York, NY 10016

METRO BOOKS and the distinctive Metro Books logo are trademarks
of Sterling Publishing Co., Inc.

© 2012 by Watkins Publishing Limited
Text © 2012 by Gerry Maguire Thompson
Artwork © 2012 by Harvey Chan and Tristan Tan/Shutterstock

This 2013 edition published by Metro Books
by arrangement with Watkins Publishing Limited.

The right of Gerry Maguire Thompson to be identified as the Author of this text has
been asserted in accordance with the Copyright, Designs and Patents Act of 1988.

All rights reserved. No part of this publication may be reproduced, stored in a retrieval system or
transmitted in any form or by any means (including electronic, mechanical, photocopying, recording,
or otherwise) without prior written permission from the publisher.

Managing Editor: Judy Barratt
Managing Designer: Suzanne Tuhrim
Production: Uzma Taj
Commissioned artwork: Harvey Chan (main animal artwork) and
Tristan Tan/Shutterstock (decorative line detail)

Typeset in Goudy Old Style and Herculanum
Color reproduction by Imagewrite

ISBN: 978-1-4351-4854-3

For information about custom editions, special sales, and premium and corporate purchases,
please contact Sterling Special Sales at 800-805-5489 or specialsales@sterlingpublishing.com

Manufactured in China

2 4 6 8 10 9 7 5 3 1

www.sterlingpublishing.com

Note:
Abbreviation used in this book:
BCE Before the Common Era (the equivalent of BC)

DEDICATION

To my beloved parents, Rev. George and Sadie Thompson,
and to all those from whom I have learned anything
about this fascinating subject.

CONTENTS

Foreword 8
How to Use This Book 10

INTRODUCTION: ABOUT CHINESE ASTROLOGY 12

The History of Chinese Astrology 14
The Five Elements 16
Yin and Yang 19
Your Astrological Make-up 20

1 THE TWELVE ANIMAL SIGNS 28

Introducing the Twelve Animal Signs 30
The Rat 32
The Ox 42
The Tiger 52
The Rabbit 62
The Dragon 72
The Snake 82
The Horse 92
The Sheep 102
The Monkey 112
The Rooster 122
The Dog 132
The Pig 142

2 RELATIONSHIPS AND COMPATIBILITY 152

Factors in Compatibility 154
The Rat in Relationships 156

The Ox in Relationships 159
The Tiger in Relationships 162
The Rabbit in Relationships 165
The Dragon in Relationships 168
The Snake in Relationships 171
The Horse in Relationships 174
The Sheep in Relationships 177
The Monkey in Relationships 180
The Rooster in Relationships 183
The Dog in Relationships 186
The Pig in Relationships 189

3 PROSPECTS OVER TIME 192

Year Influences and Your Birth Signs 194
The Year of the Rat 196
The Year of the Ox 198
The Year of the Tiger 200
The Year of the Rabbit 202
The Year of the Dragon 204
The Year of the Snake 206
The Year of the Horse 208
The Year of the Sheep 210
The Year of the Monkey 212
The Year of the Rooster 214
The Year of the Dog 216
The Year of the Pig 218

Conclusions 220
Index 221
Author's Acknowledgments 224

FOREWORD

I was first taught Chinese astrology in the late 1970s and 80s while studying macrobiotics with Oriental teachers in London, Boston and California. I found it a fascinating subject that introduced me to a way of looking at human potential that was very different from anything I had encountered to date – such as a brilliant exposition of human archetypes. I have since written a wide variety of books on personal development and mind–body–spirit matters, often drawing on the wisdom and cosmology of the Orient. It is only now, however, that I have the opportunity to draw together whatever I may have managed to learn on this subject over the last 30 and more years.

    I now make my living from helping people to get their lives to work better, and have found that astrological insights can play a very helpful part for those who wish to explore them. Studying the subject yourself can be highly transformative and empowering. I hope this book helps.

    I still find it somewhat mysterious that the movements of the planets and the cyclical passage of time should affect us in such measurable ways; yet the Chinese Zodiac system does somehow seem to work. I have never subscribed, however, to the "set-in-stone" school of astrology, which sets out highly prescribed statements and cast-iron predictions about the way you are and how things are going to be for you – all the more so when these predictions are reduced to ludicrous simplicity in downmarket tabloid horoscopes.

    Rather, I feel that it's consistent with the traditions of Chinese astrology to treat it as a highly pragmatic subject. Astrology points out tendencies and potentials, but a great deal is up to us in terms of what we make of what we may have learned about ourselves, and how we go about living subsequently. In the Introduction you will find out about the "three fates" that humanity is subject to – and only one of these is to any degree out of our control. So readers who expect to be told what's going to happen, that there's nothing they can do about it, and that no effort will be required of them, will be disappointed.

Nor is it recommended just to dip into the material presented here. For thousands of years, Chinese scholars, philosophers and even politicians have emphasized how important it is, in all matters, to look at the whole picture rather than just selected parts: traditional Chinese beliefs are the ultimate in holistic discipline. So I encourage the reader to seek to understand the whole system, rather than just finding out about your own particular animal sign or whether next year is going to be "good" or "bad". Indeed, Chinese astrology doesn't do simple "good and bad" – it's much more profound than that. Taking this bigger view will reward you with far greater insights – and a very interesting journey.

In a sense, this book is only a start to your potential study of Chinese horoscopes, and there are many aspects that could not be fitted within these pages. Nonetheless, I hope you find it valuable, interesting and rewarding.

Gerry Maguire Thompson
www.gerrymaguirethompson.com

HOW TO USE THIS BOOK

This book is a simple yet comprehensive guide to using Chinese horoscopes, which includes applying the system of 12 animal signs (see p.15) to provide insights into your character and destiny. The book offers simple explanations that are supported with charts and diagrams. You'll find the information you need to:

- explore your personality and motivations, habits and preferences, and better understand your potential for success or fulfilment in the spheres of money and wealth, career, pastimes, and health and well-being;
- discover what potential you might have for creating lasting bonds with other people – whether the relationships are in the sphere of love and romance, family, or business;
- choose the most favourable year in which to take important steps in your life, or make important decisions or changes.

HOW TO GET THE BEST RESULTS
In order to get the most out of this book, avoid the temptation to look up only the animal associated with your year of birth. According to Chinese astrology, we have many influences in our lives, each requiring consideration.

- First, read the Introduction. Not only does this part provide important background information about how the system of Chinese horoscopes developed from ancient times, it also explains all the components of your horoscope and sets out how they all work together. For example, you need to know not only about the 12-year cycle of the animal signs (this gives you the

HOW TO USE THIS BOOK

animal governing the year of your birth), but also the lunar month and the hour-of-birth cycles, as well as the cycles of the Five Elements and of yin and yang (opposing but mutually dependent forces present in all things).

- Once you have understood about the component parts of a Chinese horoscope, use the tables in the Introduction to identify which animals, Elements and energies appear in your own birth chart. You'll need to know the animal signs for your birth year, month and hour, the fixed Elements associated with each of those animals, and the mutable Element for the year of your birth.

- Armed with all this information, turn to Chapter One and learn more about the animal associated with the year of your birth. Read the general traits associated with that animal, and then find the specific analysis of the animal–Element type for your birth year. What this means will become clear in the Introduction, but, for example, if you were born in 1966 (a Horse year), you would read the general information for Horse and then the specific animal–Element type for 1966 – the Fire Horse. Finally, read how your animal influences the different spheres of your life – money, work, career, leisure and health.

- Now look up the general traits for the animals associated with the month and hour of your birth. The energetic influences of these two other signs can modify your overall character.

- Use Chapter Two to learn how all the animals in your horoscope relate to other animals in the cycle. This information will help you to work out which animal pairs offer the best potential for successful romantic and work relationships.

- Finally, in Chapter Three work out how the animals that preside over the years to come might impact on your own potential. Every year, the prevailing animal imposes a general influence – and this influence exerts its own force upon your particular personal fortunes and experiences. Use the information in this chapter to help you understand when it will be best to make decisions and changes, and when you might have to cope with challenges.

Once you've created your own horoscope readings, you can repeat the process to look at how Chinese astrology influences other people in your life.

INTRODUCTION

ABOUT CHINESE ASTROLOGY

In the West our fascination with Eastern disciplines, such as Feng Shui, has waxed and waned, but there has been continued recognition of Chinese astrology. Today, more than at any other time in history, ask others what their Chinese "animal sign" is and most will be able to tell you – even those who can't will know what you mean. In this section you'll learn how the Chinese calendar works, the origins of the animal signs and what these signs represent, and the importance of the Elements and yin and yang in the interpretation of your birth chart. At the end of the Introduction, you'll find the information you need to be able to create individual readings – begin with your own horoscope and then, when you're comfortable with the process, have a go at creating the horoscopes of your friends and family, too.

INTRODUCTION

THE HISTORY OF CHINESE ASTROLOGY

For the greater part of its history, China has developed independently of the rest of the world. This is probably why Chinese astrology has its own symbolism, its own interpretation of celestial and other influences, and its own distinctive version of the measurement of time. The major difference between the Gregorian (Western) and traditional Chinese calendars is that the latter is lunar – it's calculated according to the phases of the Moon, as well as the Earth's orbit around the Sun.

The tabulation of the lunar year is thought to date from the time of the Emperor Huang Ti, in the 27th century BCE. At first the mapping of the heavens appears to have been arbitrary, determined by general surveillance from Earth. However, by the Shang Dynasty, between the 16th and 11th centuries BCE, improved mathematical observations of the rhythms of the Sun and Moon, and of the seasons and the passage of time on Earth, had enabled Chinese astronomers to develop meticulous systems for recording celestial events. The interpretation of these events was inscribed using numerological notation onto so-called "dragon bones", dedicated shoulder blades of animals.

One overall result of the recording of astrological data was the creation of the traditional Chinese year, consisting of 12 lunar months each of 29 or 30 days. The Chinese year begins and ends later than the Gregorian year, with Chinese New Year occurring on a different date from one year to the next, usually at the end of January or beginning of February. The Chinese day is divided into two 12-hour periods, instead of the 24 consecutive hours we use in the West.

For practical purposes, the Chinese today also use the Gregorian calendar – but Chinese astrology, festivals and rituals remain lunar-based and it's the lunar calendar with which this book is concerned.

THE HISTORY OF CHINESE ASTROLOGY

ASTROLOGY AND DIVINATION

At first, Chinese astrology and astronomy were all one study. For the first 2,000 years for which we have records, astrology was used only in the divination of collective fortunes – those of the community, the state, or the agricultural year for planting, harvesting and so on. The notion of personal horoscopes came only after the arrival in China of Buddhism, which brought with it the idea that there are greater forces at work in the mapping of individual destiny.

There's no clear evidence as to how the 12 animals signs of Chinese astrology came into being. Some say the Yellow Emperor identified them around 2500BCE. However, the likeliest explanation is that early Chinese astronomers defined 12 types of human personality and assigned to each type an animal perceived as having equivalent characteristics. Chinese society was dominated by the seasons and the agricultural year, so it was in keeping for the Chinese to use a combination of wild and domesticated animals to express the diversity of human nature. The Chinese animal signs are, in order: Rat, Ox, Tiger, Rabbit, Dragon, Snake, Horse, Sheep, Monkey, Rooster, Dog, Pig. Through a process of refinement, eventually one animal became assigned to each year as the prevailing influence of that year's fortunes. This then meant that every new birth fell under the influence of one particular animal.

However, there's a great deal more to Chinese astrology than finding that we were born in the year of, for example, the Rat or the Tiger – and, of course, there are more than 12 types of people in the world. In order to explain this, Chinese astrologers developed further influencing factors, including the Five Elements (see pp.16–18), the interplay of yin and yang (see p.19), the animal sign that's in the ascendant during the hour of birth (see p.21), and the sign that influences the month of birth (see p.22).

Taking all these factors into account, astrologers created a divination system to identify our personal characteristics and our potential for a fulfilled life; our strengths and weaknesses, particularly in our ability to form relationships with others; and how the changing astrological influences could have further impact on us as we progress through our lives.

THE FIVE ELEMENTS

Throughout this book I refer to the Five Elements and their influences on each of the animal signs. In Chinese astrology, the word "element" is not used in the sense of "substance" or "material" (as with chemical elements); rather it describes a type of moderating energy. In Chinese belief the Five Elements are:

- Metal – similar to the quality of the frozen lake, the energy of Metal bestows personal characteristics such as solidity and will power.
- Water – like a river flowing around and eventually wearing down obstacles, Water bestows human qualities such as responsiveness and persuasion.
- Wood – signifying the energy that engenders life and growth (rather than the hard quality of timber itself), Wood inspires imagination and creativity.
- Fire – envisioned as leaping flames, Fire produces human qualities such as passion, and bursts of dynamic energy.
- Earth – like the settling of ashes into the ground, Earth signifies down-to-earth qualities that encourage focus on and commitment to achieving goals.

The qualities of each Element are also expressed through association with a season of the year (there are five seasons in the traditional Chinese view): Wood is associated with spring (rebirth and growth); Fire with summer (abundance and heat); Earth with late summer (cooling and settling); Metal with autumn or fall (harvest and comfort); and Water with winter (hibernation and calm).

    The 12 animal signs are each assigned one Element as a presiding "fixed" Element (see illustration, opposite) that influences that animal's characteristics. (In some schools of thought only Wood, Fire, Metal and Water are fixed; but this book has used the traditional approach that counts Earth as a fixed Element also.)

THE FIVE ELEMENTS

THE ANIMAL SIGNS AND THEIR FIXED ELEMENTS

Each animal in the cycle (named on the outer ring of this chart) is assigned its own fixed Element – Water, Wood, Fire, Metal or Earth (shown on the second ring). Furthermore, each animal–Element combination has a yin or yang orientation (innermost ring) – what this means is explained on page 19.

Each year has a "mutable" Element that may or may not be the same as the fixed Element for that year's particular animal sign. For example, the Rat's fixed Element is Water, but if you were born in 1984, the mutable Element for that year of the Rat is Wood. This means that characteristics relating to Wood can influence your life, as well as those relating to Water. Those born in 1972, though, have double Water influence, as the mutable Element for that Rat year is Water.

Each mutable Element presides over two lunar years, after which the influence transfers to the next Element in the cycle. The tables on pages 25–7 show which Element is attached to each year of birth; then, in Chapter One, detailed analysis is given for every possible animal–Element type. For example, the information on the Rat examines the characteristics of the Rat in general, and also of the Water Rat, Wood Rat, Fire Rat, Metal Rat and Earth Rat specifically. There are 60 different animal–Element types (the number of combinations it takes for each of the Five Elements to influence each of the 12 animal signs in turn). These make up the major 60-year cycle of the Chinese Zodiac.

The Elements are present in the month, day, hour, minute and second of your birth, too, and a skilled Chinese astrologer will try to find as many of the Five Elements as possible in your overall chart. For the purposes of self-analysis, it's enough to know the Elements for your year, month and hour of birth.

INTRODUCTION

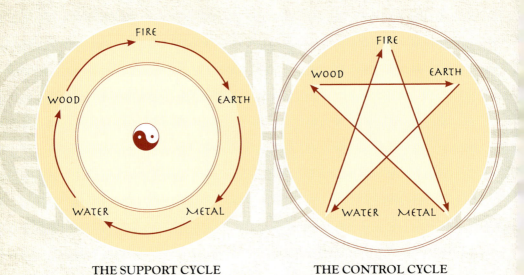

THE SUPPORT CYCLE   THE CONTROL CYCLE

CYCLES OF SUPPORT AND CONTROL

There are two cycles that describe how the Elements interact. In the Support Cycle (illustrated, above left) each Element "supports" the Element that immediately follows it in a clockwise direction. So, Metal supports Water, Water supports Wood, Wood supports Fire, Fire supports Earth and Earth supports Metal. In the Control Cycle (above right), each Element controls the Element that sits opposite it on the circle. So, Metal controls Wood, Water controls Fire, Wood controls Earth, Fire controls Metal and Earth controls Water.

    Knowing about these cycles helps us to understand the association between the Elements in our own horoscope and how they might interact to influence our characteristics. They also affect our relationships. For example, if you're in a relationship with someone born in a year ruled by the next Element on from your own, you may find that you're the one to offer support in the relationship, with your partner seeking reassurance from you. If you're in a relationship with someone whose Element is controlled by your own, you may take the lead in situations you encounter together. You'll also be influenced by the prevailing Element in each particular year. There's no judgment attached to these influences – they merely help us understand the interplay of Elements in practical terms.

YIN AND YANG

Central to all Chinese disciplines, from Feng Shui to Qi Gong, and including Chinese astrology, is the notion of yin and yang – the interaction of opposing yet complementary forces of energy. Yin and yang represent the duality in all things and in balance they create perfect harmony.

Although you may hear yang energy described as a positive force and yin as a negative, these are not value judgments – they don't mean good and bad. Rather, the terms are simple labels for the complex energies that yin and yang exert over all things. The "positive" force of yang might otherwise be thought of as light, active and dynamic; while "negative" yin energy is dark, passive and static. In practical terms this means, for example, that night and dark are considered as yin and light and day are yang; winter is yin, summer is yang.

In life, we need both forces in order to achieve balance and harmony. Too much of either yin or yang can make us feel unsettled, unhappy, or even unwell. This idea of balance in all things pervades Chinese belief. Too much or too little of anything (even something we might consider good) causes discord.

Each animal in the Chinese Zodiac is distinguished by either yin or yang qualities (I've indicated which at the start of each animal analysis in Chapter One). Knowing whether your sign is more yin or more yang helps you to understand much about the animal's characteristics. It can also have a bearing on how complementary two signs can be in a relationship – a relationship between a yin personality and a yang personality is complementary; whereas two yin or two yang personalities might not balance each other out as well. (However, this is only one factor in a relationship, and it must be put in the context of the most compelling relationship factor – that is, how the animal signs and their respective Elements combine, all covered in Chapter Two.)

INTRODUCTION

YOUR ASTROLOGICAL MAKE-UP

The Chinese believe that the most important influence over your life is the animal sign for the year in which you were born. However, animal signs appear in two other major aspects of your astrological chart, too. There's an animal relating to your month of birth (see table, p.22), and also an animal relating to your hour of birth (see diagram, opposite below). Furthermore, the animal that presides during the present year exerts its energies. This is important because how that animal interacts with the animals already present in your horoscope modifies your characteristics and has the potential to shape your fortunes. We shall look at the detail of this in Chapter Three.

THE CYCLE OF INFLUENCE
The full cycle of influence in Chinese astrology lasts 60 years (the time it takes for each of the 12 signs to be governed by each of the Five Elements; see p.17). This major cycle begins with the year of the Rat and ends with the year of the Pig. The diagram opposite shows segments of two 60-year cycles, with the animal sign, yin or yang value and Element given for each year shown.

YOUR HOROSCOPE
Before you can use the rest of this book to gain insight into your own character, relationships and well-being, and to make predictions for your future, you need to work out your personal horoscope using the following steps.

1 *Find the animal sign for your year of birth*
   Look at the tables on pages 25–7 and find the year of your birth. Note that if you were born between mid-January and mid-February, you may fall either side

YOUR ASTROLOGICAL MAKE-UP

THE 60-YEAR CYCLE

Each year of the 60-year cycle is governed by a different combination of animal sign, Element, and yin or yang energy. The animals occur five times each within each 60-year cycle, with a different governing Element each time. Here we show selected sequences of two adjacent 60-year cycles.

THE HOURS OF BIRTH

The animal influence over your hour of birth represents how others view you. Each two-hour period on the 24-hour clock is governed by a different animal sign, known as your ascendant or "rising sign", as illustrated in the wheel diagram, right.

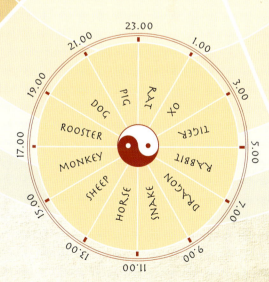

INTRODUCTION

THE LUNAR MONTHS
Each lunar month is governed by a different animal sign that exerts influence over your primary animal sign (that of the year of your birth). Knowing the animal associated with your month of birth can help you to understand the moderating influences in your character with regard to your relationships.

JANUARY 21 – FEBRUARY 19	TIGER
FEBRUARY 20 – MARCH 20	RABBIT
MARCH 21 – APRIL 19	DRAGON
APRIL 20 – MAY 20	SNAKE
MAY 21 – JUNE 21	HORSE
JUNE 22 – JULY 21	SHEEP
JULY 22 – AUGUST 21	MONKEY
AUGUST 22 – SEPTEMBER 22	ROOSTER
SEPTEMBER 23 – OCTOBER 22	DOG
OCTOBER 23 – NOVEMBER 21	PIG
NOVEMBER 22 – DECEMBER 21	RAT
DECEMBER 22 – JANUARY 20	OX

of Chinese New Year, in which case take special care to ensure you're reading from the correct year. Remember that this sign also has a corresponding fixed Element – you can look this up in the diagram on page 17.

2 **Find the Element that applies to the year in which you were born**
Once you've found the animal that applies to the year of your birth, read across the same line to find the corresponding Element. This is your mutable Element and it moderates your animal traits.

3 **Find the animal that governs your lunar month of birth**
The table above provides you with the animal sign that governs the month of your birth. This sign can be an important influence in your relationships, especially with your parents, children, teachers and those in authority. It can also offer retrospective insight into your childhood characteristics.

4 **Work out your Chinese "rising sign"**
Your "rising sign" (or ascendant) is the animal sign that governs the two-hour period covering your time of birth (local time). Find your rising sign from the diagram on page 21. This sign represents aspects of yourself that can seem to come out of nowhere to surprise those who know you, and even yourself.

YOUR ASTROLOGICAL MAKE-UP

Note down all the animals and the Elements in your astrological make-up, making sure you indicate which components relate to which aspect of your birth chart (that is, the year, month and hour of birth). Then, use the rest of the book to find out how all the components influence your character, relationships and destiny.

BALANCE, HARMONY AND COMPATIBILITY

Each of the three animal signs – for your year, month and hour of birth – enables you to learn something about your character. Chinese astrology emphasizes the importance of how the animals and their corresponding Elements in this composite horoscope interact with one another to create a whole picture. In the Chinese view, the ideal combination is one that provides balance and avoids extremes. So an "ideal" chart includes a range of animals that can find harmony with one another with a selection of Elements that support one another. Chapter One gives detailed analysis for each of the animals and their Elements, while Chapter Two, on relationships, helps you to assess the degree of compatibility between your horoscope and the horoscopes of your friends and family.

FATE, DESTINY AND INDIVIDUAL INTERPRETATION

Each of us is unique and it's obvious that even two people who share the same combination of birth year, month, hour and Element influences won't have exactly the same character traits. The Chinese believe that astrological make-up is only one of three fates that make each of us who we are. Astrology provides the Heaven Fate, which is immutable, dictated by the specific time of your birth. However, we are also subject to individualizing factors, such as the place of our birth and where we live now. The Chinese call this our Earth Fate and it's to a certain degree mutable – where we choose to reside, for example, is something we can control. Finally, our upbringing, parental influences, life experiences and the choices we make about how to live our lives all contribute to our own subtle uniqueness. This is known as our Human or Self Fate and it's more or less entirely within our control. Our own expectations, beliefs and attitudes are all part of Self Fate and will themselves specifically influence our potential.

INTRODUCTION

Although Heaven Fate is immutable, it's by no means binding. The traditional Chinese view is that we can crucially affect our astrological influences by the ways in which we take charge of and manage our Self Fate – what we make of the opportunities and circumstances with which we're faced. For these reasons, when you interpret the astrological indications of your Chinese horoscope, think of them as tendencies and possible outcomes, rather than as cast-iron destiny. While astrology can never fix your fate, understanding the complex and ever-changing interplay of influences in your horoscope over time will certainly help you to make the most of your potential, and to adapt to new and unexpected circumstances.

GOOD FORTUNE

In Chinese astrology, the concept of so-called "good fortune" is not simplistic, fatalistic or superstitious, nor is it bestowed upon someone purely as a result of astrological influences. Achieving good results in life depends on applying the potential your horoscope suggests for you, and on making sure that you conduct yourself in ways that show respect and consideration for others. To put it in the most basic terms, we might say that although the heavenly bodies cast their influence over our lives, in the end we make our own luck.

GUIDELINES FOR LIVING

Chinese astrology embodies a number of traditional philosophical principles for the way in which we should live, regardless of our horoscope. In stark contrast to our consumer society, Chinese philosophy advocates that personal happiness and fulfilment come through making the most of our unique potential and individual strengths and minimizing the effects of our shortcomings. Furthermore, we should try to be true to ourselves and our nature, and to nurture and cherish family life as well as the society in which we live. In Chinese belief every person, with his or her unique traits, is essential to a diverse and capable community. Through awareness of these principles and adherence to them, the Chinese believe we're more able to produce the best results for our own lives.

YOUR ASTROLOGICAL MAKE-UP

TABLE FOR YEAR OF BIRTH, ELEMENT AND DATES

Use this chart to calculate your year-of-birth animal sign, together with the prevailing mutable Element. The chart also enables you to work out the animal that presides over the particular year you're in now.

YEAR AND DATE	ELEMENT	SIGN
FEBRUARY 19, 1939 – FEBRUARY 7, 1940	EARTH	RABBIT
FEBRUARY 8, 1940 – JANUARY 26, 1941	METAL	DRAGON
JANUARY 27, 1941 – FEBRUARY 14, 1942	METAL	SNAKE
FEBRUARY 15, 1942 – FEBRUARY 3, 1943	WATER	HORSE
FEBRUARY 4, 1943 – JANUARY 24, 1944	WATER	SHEEP
JANUARY 25, 1944 – FEBRUARY 11, 1945	WOOD	MONKEY
FEBRUARY 12, 1945 – FEBRUARY 1, 1946	WOOD	ROOSTER
FEBRUARY 2, 1946 – JANUARY 21, 1947	FIRE	DOG
JANUARY 22, 1947 – FEBRUARY 9, 1948	FIRE	PIG
FEBRUARY 10, 1948 – JANUARY 28, 1949	EARTH	RAT
JANUARY 29, 1949 – FEBRUARY 15, 1950	EARTH	OX
FEBRUARY 16, 1950 – FEBRUARY 5, 1951	METAL	TIGER
FEBRUARY 6, 1951 – JANUARY 25, 1952	METAL	RABBIT
JANUARY 26, 1952 – FEBRUARY 13, 1953	WATER	DRAGON
FEBRUARY 14, 1953 – FEBRUARY 2, 1954	WATER	SNAKE
FEBRUARY 3, 1954 – JANUARY 23, 1955	WOOD	HORSE
JANUARY 24, 1955 – FEBRUARY 10, 1956	WOOD	SHEEP
FEBRUARY 11, 1956 – JANUARY 29, 1957	FIRE	MONKEY
JANUARY 30, 1957 – FEBRUARY 17, 1958	FIRE	ROOSTER
FEBRUARY 18, 1958 – FEBRUARY 6, 1959	EARTH	DOG
FEBRUARY 7, 1959 – JANUARY 27, 1960	EARTH	PIG
JANUARY 28, 1960 – FEBRUARY 14, 1961	METAL	RAT
FEBRUARY 15, 1961 – FEBRUARY 4, 1962	METAL	OX
FEBRUARY 5, 1962 – JANUARY 24, 1963	WATER	TIGER
JANUARY 25, 1963 – FEBRUARY 12, 1964	WATER	RABBIT
FEBRUARY 13, 1964 – JANUARY 31, 1965	WOOD	DRAGON
FEBRUARY 1, 1965 – JANUARY 20, 1966	WOOD	SNAKE
JANUARY 21, 1966 – FEBRUARY 8, 1967	FIRE	HORSE

INTRODUCTION

FEBRUARY 9, 1967 – JANUARY 28, 1968	FIRE	SHEEP
JANUARY 29, 1968 – FEBRUARY 15, 1969	EARTH	MONKEY
FEBRUARY 16, 1969 – FEBRUARY 5, 1970	EARTH	ROOSTER
FEBRUARY 6, 1970 – JANUARY 25, 1971	METAL	DOG
JANUARY 26, 1971 – FEBRUARY 14, 1972	METAL	PIG
FEBRUARY 15, 1972 – FEBRUARY 2, 1973	WATER	RAT
FEBRUARY 3, 1973 – JANUARY 23, 1974	WATER	OX
JANUARY 24, 1974 – FEBRUARY 10, 1975	WOOD	TIGER
FEBRUARY 11, 1975 – JANUARY 30, 1976	WOOD	RABBIT
JANUARY 31, 1976 – FEBRUARY 17, 1977	FIRE	DRAGON
FEBRUARY 18, 1977 – FEBRUARY 6, 1978	FIRE	SNAKE
FEBRUARY 7, 1978 – JANUARY 27, 1979	EARTH	HORSE
JANUARY 28, 1979 – FEBRUARY 15, 1980	EARTH	SHEEP
FEBRUARY 16, 1980 – FEBRUARY 4, 1981	METAL	MONKEY
FEBRUARY 5, 1981 – JANUARY 24, 1982	METAL	ROOSTER
JANUARY 25, 1982 – FEBRUARY 12, 1983	WATER	DOG
FEBRUARY 13, 1983 – FEBRUARY 1, 1984	WATER	PIG
FEBRUARY 2, 1984 – FEBRUARY 19, 1985	WOOD	RAT
FEBRUARY 20, 1985 – FEBRUARY 8, 1986	WOOD	OX
FEBRUARY 9, 1986 – JANUARY 28, 1987	FIRE	TIGER
JANUARY 29, 1987 – FEBRUARY 16, 1988	FIRE	RABBIT
FEBRUARY 17, 1988 – FEBRUARY 5, 1989	EARTH	DRAGON
FEBRUARY 6, 1989 – JANUARY 25, 1990	EARTH	SNAKE
JANUARY 26, 1990 – FEBRUARY 13, 1991	METAL	HORSE
FEBRUARY 14, 1991 – FEBRUARY 2, 1992	METAL	SHEEP
FEBRUARY 3, 1992 – JANUARY 21, 1993	WATER	MONKEY
JANUARY 22, 1993 – FEBRUARY 9, 1994	WATER	ROOSTER
FEBRUARY 10, 1994 – JANUARY 30, 1995	WOOD	DOG
JANUARY 31, 1995 – FEBRUARY 18, 1996	WOOD	PIG
FEBRUARY 19, 1996 – FEBRUARY 6, 1997	FIRE	RAT
FEBRUARY 7, 1997 – JANUARY 27, 1998	FIRE	OX
JANUARY 28, 1998 – FEBRUARY 15, 1999	EARTH	TIGER
FEBRUARY 16, 1999 – FEBRUARY 4, 2000	EARTH	RABBIT

YOUR ASTROLOGICAL MAKE-UP

FEBRUARY 5, 2000 – JANUARY 23, 2001	METAL	DRAGON
JANUARY 24, 2001 – FEBRUARY 11, 2002	METAL	SNAKE
FEBRUARY 12, 2002 – JANUARY 31, 2003	WATER	HORSE
FEBRUARY 1, 2003 – JANUARY 20, 2004	WATER	SHEEP
JANUARY 21, 2004 – FEBRUARY 8, 2005	WOOD	MONKEY
FEBRUARY 9, 2005 – JANUARY 28, 2006	WOOD	ROOSTER
JANUARY 29, 2006 – FEBRUARY 16, 2007	FIRE	DOG
FEBRUARY 17, 2007 – FEBRUARY 6, 2008	FIRE	PIG
FEBRUARY 7, 2008 – JANUARY 25, 2009	EARTH	RAT
JANUARY 26, 2009 – FEBRUARY 13 2010	EARTH	OX
FEBRUARY 14, 2010 – FEBRUARY 2, 2011	METAL	TIGER
FEBRUARY 3, 2011 – JANUARY 22, 2012	METAL	RABBIT
JANUARY 23, 2012 – FEBRUARY 9, 2013	WATER	DRAGON
FEBRUARY 10, 2013 – JANUARY 30, 2014	WATER	SNAKE
JANUARY 31, 2014 – FEBRUARY 18, 2015	WOOD	HORSE
FEBRUARY 19, 2015 – FEBRUARY 7, 2016	WOOD	SHEEP
FEBRUARY 8, 2016 – JANUARY 27, 2017	FIRE	MONKEY
JANUARY 28, 2017 – FEBRUARY 15, 2018	FIRE	ROOSTER
FEBRUARY 16, 2018 – FEBRUARY 4, 2019	EARTH	DOG
FEBRUARY 5, 2019 – JANUARY 24, 2020	EARTH	PIG
JANUARY 25, 2020 – FEBRUARY 11, 2021	METAL	RAT
FEBRUARY 12, 2021 – JANUARY 31, 2022	METAL	OX
FEBRUARY 1, 2022 – JANUARY 21, 2023	WATER	TIGER
JANUARY 22, 2023 – FEBRUARY 9, 2024	WATER	RABBIT
FEBRUARY 10, 2024 – JANUARY 28, 2025	WOOD	DRAGON
JANUARY 29, 2025 – FEBRUARY 16, 2026	WOOD	SNAKE
FEBRUARY 17, 2026 – FEBRUARY 5, 2027	FIRE	HORSE
FEBRUARY 6, 2027 – JANUARY 25, 2028	FIRE	SHEEP
JANUARY 26, 2028 – FEBRUARY 12, 2029	EARTH	MONKEY
FEBRUARY 13, 2029 – FEBRUARY 2, 2030	EARTH	ROOSTER
FEBRUARY 3, 2030 – JANUARY 22, 2031	METAL	DOG
JANUARY 23, 2031 – FEBRUARY 10, 2032	METAL	PIG
FEBRUARY 11, 2032 – JANUARY 30, 2033	WATER	RAT

CHAPTER ONE

THE TWELVE ANIMAL SIGNS

Ancient Chinese astrologers drew upon the traits of 12 animals – some wild, some domesticated – brilliantly and elegantly to summarize 12 key human archetypes. In this section all 12 animal signs are given comprehensive treatment to reveal not just the general personality traits they represent, but also how each of the Five Elements modifies those characteristics to create, in all, 60 specific sub-types of human nature. Discover how the animal types deal with their career and money and with their relationships with other people. Learn how they express their inner selves through their tastes and preferences, and how their constitutions are revealed in their health and well-being. And remember: you have a particular animal sign not only for your year of birth, but for your month and hour of birth, too, so you can apply the information in this chapter to all three categories of your horoscope.

INTRODUCING THE TWELVE ANIMAL SIGNS

From the Rat to the Pig and the Snake to the Sheep, the qualities of each animal sign of the Chinese Zodiac are often at odds with Western stereotypes – for example, while the rat may be considered vermin and a scavenger in the West, for the Chinese it is instead an animal of imagination and ingenuity. Chinese astrology challenges us to reassess our associations and consider both the positive and the negative potential in each animal archetype.

When you look up your horoscope, bear in mind the potential you have for both positive and negative traits. You might be tempted to think that you would rather be a Tiger or a Dragon than a Rabbit or a Monkey, but in Chinese astrology no animal is inherently better than any other – every type can be happy or unhappy, fulfilled or unfulfilled, successful or unsuccessful, in a healthy or unhealthy relationship; and each one can make a valuable contribution to society – or not, depending upon how they live life. Rather than wishing you had been born under the influence of a different animal archetype, consider how you can make the most of your particular potential, use your traits to build positive relationships with others, and moderate the negative aspects of your persona.

Consider, too, the many different animal aspects of your personality. Although the single most important animal in your horoscope is the one relating to the year of your birth, it's too simplistic to think that this is the only animal that has influence over you. Who you are is reflected in the animals associated with the month and the hour of your birth, too. In the Introduction, you learned which animals these are, and here you can learn about each animal's traits in relation to money and career; tastes and preferences; and health and well-being.

In this chapter detailed analysis of each of the 12 animal signs will help you to decode your own personality traits in light of which animal is associated with

INTRODUCING THE TWELVE ANIMAL SIGNS

the year and hour of your birth. You'll learn about your animal "pair" – the animal that plays yin to your yang, or vice versa, because each of the 12 animal signs has an opposite number with characteristics to complement, enhance and even fulfil your own.

Chinese astrology also places emphasis on the influences of the Five Elements, giving each animal type five sub-types, according to which of the Five Elements is associated with that animal's year. Some Elements will tend to moderate some of the typical qualities of an animal sign, while others may exaggerate them. And for each animal sign, one of the Five Element variations will experience a double influence, because the Element for that particular year is the same as the Fixed Element for one of the signs. For example, the Fixed Element for the Tiger sign is Wood. If you were born in 1974 – a year that gives the Wood Tiger – you'll have double Wood influence.

The point of all this is to illustrate how we must always bear in mind that each of us is subject to a complex combination of many different influences. In the process of deciphering these influences, we can start to work past the generalizations of astrology and home in on some of the detail.

Finally, the animal sign for the current year will influence your behaviour, your personality and your experiences. For example, a Rat year can bring people of all signs some experience of Rat energies. In Chapter Three we examine how each sign impacts on your fortunes when its turn of the wheel comes around, once every 12 years.

If you're not yet sure which sign you were born under, the opening page for each sign in this chapter lists the years associated with that sign. Remember that if you were born in January or February, you'll need to note the Oriental year start dates (see pp.25–7) to be sure which animal year you were born in.

When you've decoded your own personality and learned about how Chinese astrology influences your own life, you can use the information to better understand people close to you – your partner, family members or close friends. Chinese astrologers believe that in order fully to understand your world, you must become aware of the characteristics of all the animal types around you.

THE TWELVE ANIMAL SIGNS | 鼠

THE RAT

RAT YEARS: 1900, 1912, 1924, 1936, 1948, 1960, 1972, 1984, 1996, 2008, 2020, 2032
RAT HOURS: 2300–0100
FIXED ELEMENT: WATER   YANG SIGN

As a Water sign, the Rat person is adaptable, imaginative and ingenious, quickly responding to new situations to spot their potential and take advantage of them. Just as water meanders around obstacles in its path, always flowing downhill to the sea, so the Rat responds empathetically to the circumstances it encounters, finding intuitive ways to reach its goals. A born survivor, the Rat never runs out of options.

Despite being quick and bright, and brimming with new ideas, the Rat is also easily distracted and may not always put his or her ideas fully into practice before moving on. Scattered energies aside, the Rat is tenacious with strong entrepreneurial abilities, and is intolerant of waste, laziness or inefficiency. A liking for control or power can make the Rat exploitative as a leader, and the Rat's ambitious nature can sometimes be a weakness. Beware a Rat under threat – when nervous, he or she can turn nasty.

At ease in any group situation, the Rat may be something of a party animal and always knows what's going on in the neighbourhood. However, Rats closely guard their own privacy: this animal is always looking out for Number One.

The Rat's complementary and opposite sign is the Ox.

KEYWORDS
• ENERGETIC • ACTIVE • CREATIVE • INNOVATIVE • CHARMING
• INSIGHTFUL • AMBITIOUS • CLEVER • OBSERVANT • RESOURCEFUL
• GREGARIOUS • DEVIOUS • ACQUISITIVE • FICKLE • PICKY

THE FIVE TYPES OF RAT

METAL RAT: 1900, 1960, 2020
"Rat on the Roof-beam"
The Element of Metal sharpens and adds structure, focus and organizational ability to the Rat's resourcefulness. Metal also strengthens the lungs and large intestine – the organ system associated with this Element.

Strong-willed and single-minded, the Metal Rat has a clear sense of purpose driven by energy, dynamism and a need for physical activity. A dominant individual, perhaps lacking diplomacy, this outspoken Rat puts plans into practice with enviable self-confidence.

Anger, jealousy, passion and sensuality are some of the intense emotions associated with this Rat. The Metal Rat may obscure or withhold them, and may have a tendency to become destructive. Metal Rats would do well to remember that the best relationships work on compromise and that being less intense is not necessarily a sign of weakness or of a lack of commitment to their own aims.

A sincere, moral and idealistic person, the Metal Rat is concerned for the well-being of others, but is nonetheless motivated also by self-interest. The Metal Rat can make money from anything that's to hand, which is just as well as he or she has expensive tastes and enjoys both spending and investing.

A keen home-maker, the Metal Rat may particularly enjoy decorating his or her environment, making it as impressive as possible.

WATER RAT: 1912, 1972, 2032
"Rat on the Mountain"
A double helping of Water gives Rats born in 1912 and 1972 especially acute powers of insight and of mental agility. Water Rats are able to gather knowledge and self-educate, as well as to try everything out until they find a winding way

THE RAT 鼠

through any problem. Powerful communicators with intuitive and empathetic understanding of others, these Rats tend to be more flexible than other types and more able to tolerate the desires and objectives of other people. They have a strong interest in helping others. Like a still lake, this Rat is generally calmer and more serene, less passionate and less driven than other Rats.

Able to listen to, relate to and influence other people, Water Rats are on the whole well-liked and respected. They're diplomatic and less confrontational than other Rats, and more prepared to go with the flow. However, this is still a Rat – shrewd and perceptive, the Water Rat knows how to engage people to help his or her own cause, using good relations to further his or her own purpose.

With double Water influence, Water Rats are particularly susceptible to problems with the kidneys and urinary system (the organ system of the Water Element), and should carefully monitor their salt intake. They should also protect their essential energy, or *chi*, against excessive damage through stress. The Water Rat is well advised, when under pressure, to let down his or her instinctive guard a little, to share feelings and worries with others and to enlist support from them.

WOOD RAT: 1924, 1984
"Rat on the Roof"

The Wood Element is associated with the season of spring, which makes this Rat bright, sensitive, artistic and creative, with a special interest in harmony and beauty. Especially alert, a Wood Rat may turn his or her mind to different things at the same time – although this does sometimes emphasize the Rat's general tendency to become easily distracted. When considering new ventures, the Wood Rat is perhaps a little more cautious than other Rat types and usually ends up working harder to achieve the same results.

All Rat types appear to be self-confident, but Wood Rats are in fact surprisingly prone to worry – something that may be discerned only by those closest to them. The sensitive Wood Rat benefits greatly from the love and security provided by close friends and family. Showing less bravado than other Rats, Wood Rats may be generally better-liked, while their thoughtful, more discerning natures makes them better able to lead others (always with underlying self-interest, of course). Wood Rats love to help others and are generous with the time they will dedicate to doing so, which can mean they may sometimes take on too much – especially as they're also keen to gain approval and maintain an impression of being in complete command.

Negative energy, or *chi*, flowing through the liver or gall bladder – the organs related to the Wood Element – can make the Wood Rat prone to anger, impatience or excessive control. In order to protect these organs, and balance this energy, the Wood Rat should avoid greasy foods and too much alcohol, and eat plenty of light foods such as leafy green vegetables – the special foods of spring.

Wood Rats are most at home among trees and vegetation, and need to find artistic pursuits that indulge their creativity. With plant life around them and an outlet for their artistic natures, Wood Rats are less likely to become anxious or suffer from temper, and more likely to achieve their full potential in life.

FIRE RAT: 1936, 1996
"Rat in the Field"

The excitable energy of the Fire Element makes this the most dynamic Rat type, exuding energy, enthusiasm, sociability and impulsiveness. An inquisitive nature and pervading interest in transformation, movement and travel mean that the Fire Rat can be the most independent and competitive of all Rat types.

Try to keep a Fire Rat cooped up or make him or her conform and this Rat will do exactly the opposite – jumping up and scuttling off in another direction. Fire Rats are averse to routine, and will seek out change – in home, work, friends or leisure pursuits. They have an infectious enthusiasm for life and love mixing with other people, both socially and at work, which makes them engaging motivators, great at enlisting others and at leading them. The general Rat tendency to help others manifests in the Fire Rat as a need to be absorbed in philanthropic campaigns, displaying generosity and chivalry. However, Fire Rats can be hot-headed communicators, offering up their opinions using blunt or overbearing language that can lack sensitivity and may alienate others. Led by their hearts, rather than their heads, these Rats can appear to lack self-discipline, but they're generally high achievers.

The organ system of the Fire Element is the heart, making low-fat foods and regular exercise important to the Fire Rat's well-being. To be consistently successful and fulfilled in life, Fire Rats are well advised to cultivate patience – both to stick at their goals in order to achieve them, and to deal with other people who may well be less dynamic and self-assured than they are.

EARTH RAT: 1948, 2008
"Rat in the Granary"

The Earth Element brings stability, solidity and rootedness to this Rat type. Compared with other Rats, Earth Rats may display more conservative natures (leading them to crave security), and greater levels of common sense and realism, as well as an ability to live in the moment. They prefer to stay in one place as much as possible, and – unusually for a Rat – to focus on a single project at a time.

Generally more prudent and risk-averse, Earth Rats are less interested in dubious, self-serving interactions than other Rat types, making them less prone to the resulting highs and lows in fortune. However, Earth Rats should avoid being overly cautious or acquiescent, as this can lead to long deliberations that cause them to miss out on some of life's opportunities. Earth Rats work consistently to create contentment and a secure future for themselves and their families, steadily accumulating material wealth. However, a tendency to look after their own may make the Earth Rat appear less outwardly generous than some of the other Rats.

Reputation and image are important to an Earth Rat, and this may seem self-serving; but coupled with the Rat's general interest in helping others, the Earth Rat is able to forge and maintain positive relationships. The Earth Rat's tendency to set up home in one place inevitably reinforces the strength of his or her friendships, making Earth Rats warm, loyal companions.

The organs associated with the Earth Element are the spleen, stomach and pancreas. As a result, Earth Rats who eat too many carbohydrates and sweet foods are prone to weight gain and, in extreme cases, diabetes.

WORK, CAREER AND MONEY

Ambitious; Intelligent; Innovative; Versatile; Hardworking

THE RAT IN WORK AND CAREER

With their clever, quick and sharp minds, Rats have a legendary ability to assess situations speedily and intuitively, distinguish what are the key problems and issues, make accurate judgments, produce instinctive strategies and then overcome obstacles in the implementation of their solutions.

Although Rats may have several careers over a lifetime, they're generally ambitious, greatly enjoying power and prestige. Their shrewd natures mean they're never slow to detect opportunities that may help them move forward, although their tendencies toward deviousness can mean they have to work hard to earn others' trust, especially those with whom they're trying to strike a deal.

Happy to take the lead, Rats tend to be happier in the role of boss than employee, making excellent advisors, consultants and managers. They enjoy independence, flexibility and variety; and they don't easily tolerate routine. The combination of these factors makes Rats well-disposed for self-employment. Rats can happily juggle several tasks or jobs at one time, and being under-used or inactive makes them nervous and on edge. The Rat employee is the one who comes asking for responsibility or tasks to take on. As bosses, Rats are caring about their staff, but their shrewd natures materialize during salary reviews, when employees may find pay rises hard to come by.

COMMON CAREER POSSIBILITIES
• JOURNALISM • WRITING • INVESTIGATION • COMMUNICATIONS
• RESEARCHER • CONSULTANT • COUNSELLOR • MANAGER • SALESPERSON
• ADMINISTRATOR • POLITICIAN • ENGINEER • MUSICIAN

THE RAT AND MONEY

Money is important to the Rat. Acquisitive and good at finding opportunities to make money, the Rat certainly doesn't then like to be parted from it. Rats are good at keeping track of their accounts, too, and can dispense excellent financial advice to other people. They're good savers and hoarders, constantly putting something by for when times are harder – and they're also very good at finding clever and creative ways to deal with financial hardship.

Rats are well known for being thrifty and frugal – penny-pinching even. They hate waste and don't like throwing things away, and will always try to save money by finding uses for old items rather than dumping them. This can get out of hand at times – the Rat's storage space may well become filled to the brim with items they're keeping "just in case". Nor can Rats resist a bargain, even when the usefulness of or need for the item is questionable.

Although the traditional Chinese reputation enjoyed by Rats is one of stinginess, this particular cultural and historical reference tells only part of the story. In fact, Rats withhold generosity only from those they dislike. Otherwise they can be generous, especially toward their nearest and dearest – their close friends and their children and other dependents in particular. Furthermore, that generosity may well take the form of something other than gifts that money can buy. Their generosity is just as likely to be demonstrated in a gift of kindness.

Nevertheless, greed is definitely a possibility for the Rat, who may alienate others as a result of his or her need to keep accumulating financial wealth. So great is the Rat's need to acquire money that he or she may be tempted into some dodgy dealing, or even gambling. However, despite their enviable perception and insight and their clear ability to turn insight into financial wherewithal, Rats do not make good gamblers, and would be well advised to resist the urge to speculate. Even the best gamblers lose at least some of the time, and the Rat hates losing money, so when this happens he or she can suffer disproportionate regret and morbid self-recrimination.

And what does the Rat like to spend his or her money on? Having a good time, of course! Food, drink and entertainment are top of the Rat's wish list.

鼠 | THE TWELVE ANIMAL SIGNS

PREFERENCES AND WELL-BEING

Living life in the fast lane

PEOPLE, TASTES AND PASTIMES

Rat people enjoy the good things in life. They're notoriously outgoing and gregarious and they have lots of friends to chat to and socialize with. They're inquisitive and curious, not to say nosy and prone to gossiping. Their quick minds enable them to pick up on subtle signals and snippets of information that they deftly put together to extrapolate the overall picture of a situation – often with great accuracy and insight. However, despite their love of gossip, they tend to be secretive about their own lives, playing their cards close to their chest. Highly competitive, Rats can be aggressive on occasion – a trait they would be well advised to keep under control.

Rats hate boredom. Their need for stimulation means they rarely stop still during their daily lives and it also means they enjoy travelling for its own sake. Flexibility is essential for the adventurous Rat, who looks for a holiday with plenty of activity and lots of opportunity to explore all the sights, sounds and smells of their destination. Their inquisitive natures mean they thrive on discovering new cultures and ways of life. They love to haggle over prices and will bring home an abundance of souvenirs to add to the hoards already there. Their acquisitive nature is displayed for all to see in the amount of stuff that accumulates around them.

Rats are good at home-making, and are not averse to doing domestic tasks and chores. In fact they're utterly intolerant of idleness, whether in themselves or in others. They want their home to be cosy and comfortable, and are less concerned with "showiness" or grandeur than other animal signs. Their love of family structure means that they enjoy being with their nearest and dearest, but their inherently sociable natures mean that it's also important for them to spend time with their wider clan and among their friends.

Rats have a strong tendency to over-commit their time, taking on too many activities or making too many offers of help. If they're not careful, their energies may become too scattered to be truly effective.

HEALTH AND WELL-BEING
Fixed Element: Water
The Rat's fixed Element is Water, which relates to the organs of the kidneys and bladder, and to the urinary system. Drinking enough water and watching salt intake, as well as the occasional detox, are key to the health of the kidney system.

All Rats – enjoying as they do the good things in life – may be prone to a somewhat greedy streak. They may be tempted to do, eat and drink too much, and eat rather randomly or opportunistically. This puts a strain on the digestive system and can cause acid stomach conditions. Rats are also predisposed to putting on weight later in life. Above all, Rats are well advised to try to minimize their intake of junk foods, especially as they're rarely still and so have a tendency to eat on the run, grabbing something fatty or sweet when they can.

Generally speaking, Rats are naturally active creatures with lots of energy and stamina. However, they can also be surprisingly highly strung; and prone to nervousness and fretting – although a Rat's angst may not always be obvious to outsiders. Rats tend to ignore symptoms of illness or stress and carry on with their typical Rat dynamism. Regular physical activity can help use up or dispel any pent-up nervous energy, and calming practices – such as meditation, tai chi or yoga – are good for the Rat, to help restore balance. Power naps enable Rats to quickly recharge their batteries to avoid exhaustion and restore their trademark mental and physical alertness. Rats should avoid excessive intake of stimulants, such as caffeine, and may be wise to work on maintaining strong self-discipline in order not to overindulge.

The strong family structure that is the Rat's great comfort (and that he or she takes time to build around him- or herself) provides a stable, secure, safe environment for living, and can create a positive, moderating force in the maintenance of the Rat's health and well-being.

THE OX

OX YEARS: 1901, 1913, 1925, 1937, 1949, 1961, 1973, 1985, 1997, 2009, 2021, 2033
OX HOURS: 0100–0300
FIXED ELEMENT: EARTH   **YIN SIGN**

Diligent, hardworking and dependable, the Ox gets on with the job, and has great capacity for endurance. He or she takes a systematic approach to any task and will see it through until the bitter end. The Ox person is practical, industrious, determined, methodical and down-to-earth, and also honest, straightforward and loyal: with an Ox what you see is what you get.

The Ox approaches life with a steady and calm attitude, avoiding risk and establishing firm habits. This last trait can make Oxen appear inflexible, but in fact they simply enjoy routine. Lovers of peace and quiet, they like to consider things carefully and come to firm conclusions.

The self-reliant Ox is not at ease with authority, becoming sulky if he or she is forced to act against instincts. Oxen make good friends but bad enemies – when provoked, they may lose their tempers and become aggressive and dangerous. Most Ox people would be well advised to lighten up from time to time in order to get on better with those around them. Home is of central importance to all five types of Ox. This animal sign wants to build foundations for a secure and prosperous future, and this pervades everything the Ox does, says and thinks.

The Ox's complementary and opposite sign is the Rat.

KEYWORDS
• RELIABLE • LOYAL • HONEST • SINCERE • HARDWORKING
• PERFECTIONIST • QUIET • TRUTHFUL • COMMITTED • OBSTINATE
• WILFUL • CAUTIOUS • HABITUAL • RIGID

THE FIVE TYPES OF OX

METAL OX: 1901, 1961, 2021
"Ox on the Road"
The highly motivated Metal Ox is a force to be reckoned with. Metal enhances the Ox's innate attributes, bringing extra toughness, tenacity, determination and strength of purpose, and even a degree of austerity. This type of Ox may be prone to jealousy and can sometimes take him- or herself too seriously.

This Ox has the greatest potential for stubbornness of all 60 of the animal sign variations, with a "do or die" attitude to their pursuits. No wonder they sometimes appear arrogant and unyielding! Those born under the auspices of the Metal Ox are well advised to try hard to keep an open mind.

You can expect to hear exactly what the Metal Ox wants to say, without any sugar-coating. This type of Ox expresses his or her views simply and strongly, sometimes leading to serious clashes. Those around the Metal Ox, however, should try not to take offence – any insensitivity is an unintentional by-product of this animal sign's straightforward nature.

All that said, the Metal Ox is loyal, responsible and dependable. He or she is also more passionate and humorous than other Ox types, and has a deep sense of morality, believing in justice and the traditional values that set out right from wrong. Metal Oxen enjoy study and apply themselves assiduously to this activity, although it's the practical application of their learning that most interests them – they're not as readily engaged by anything theoretical or abstract.

WATER OX: 1913, 1973, 2033
"Ox at the Gate"
Water has a moderating effect on some of the more extreme qualities of the Ox, creating a more fluid and flexible and quicker-thinking prototype. The Water

THE OX 牛

Ox is more patient and more tactically aware than the Ox standard. Although Oxen are generally poor communicators, the Water Ox can be articulate and makes a better listener than other types.

Methodical, practical and organized, like most Ox types, the Water Ox is also innovative and comparatively flexible. Rather than merely plodding ahead, determinedly pushing through obstacles to an end goal, this Ox type has intuition and foresight and is willing to take steps to prevent problems in the first place.

The Ox is always looking to strengthen his or her position and stature, but in the Water Ox this ambitious nature is rooted in a more realistic and responsive take on the potential in any given situation. Water Oxen tend to be less single-minded and stubborn, and better able simultaneously to pursue multiple objectives, and even to strike out in new directions when necessary.

More easy-going than other Oxen, the Water Ox is a relatively sensitive soul, who needs to express his or her own feelings and shows concern for others' ideas and emotions. He or she welcomes give and take, and this co-operative nature manifests in a more open-minded attitude to the contributions of others. In the workplace this makes the Water Ox a valuable employee, who is fiercely hardworking, but open to compromise, and also motivated to look after weaker individuals in a team.

WOOD OX: 1925, 1985
"Ox from the Sea"

This more relaxed type of Ox has more emotional warmth than others in the clan. He or she is more likely to respond appropriately to a given situation, rather than ploughing on through it, and others find him or her easier to "read" and respond to. The Wood Ox is probably the least obstinate of all the Oxen, and is the most open-minded, creative and open to change.

A more tolerant and socially adept Ox type, the Wood Ox has a strong interest in his or her surroundings, and the world at large, and is more able to empathize with the cultures and beliefs of others. Co-operative team players, Wood Oxen have an acute sense of fair play and are loyal, ethical and principled.

They tend to show concern for the well-being of others and for society as a whole; and they have a sense of service. As a result, they soon earn the respect and admiration of those around them.

However, this doesn't mean that the Wood Ox lacks the same strong sense of drive as the other Ox types. Rather, Wood Oxen apply their drive to objectives that are perhaps less self-serving: they're more able to set goals in the context of the wider scheme of things. They tend to be confident and are naturally authoritative and good at speaking up for themselves, but they're also good at being leaders and representing others. They do, however, have a temper, which can be very quickly sparked off. One way to balance these negative energies is for them to look after the liver system (the organ system of the Wood Element) by moderating their intake of alcohol and rich foods.

Among the Oxen, the Wood Ox is the most refined, tending to be tasteful, artistic and creative – the hallmark of the Wood Element. Intolerant of chaos and lack of order, Wood Oxen enjoy the aesthetics of their surroundings.

FIRE OX: 1937, 1997
"Ox in the Lake"

Relatively quick, dynamic and impulsive, the Fire Ox is a spirited person with bigger dreams – and more of them – than the other Oxen. His or her fiery temperament can lead to great effectiveness, but it's not without its pitfalls.

With Fire burning away on top of the Ox family's basic determination, tenacity and need for control, Fire Oxen are highly self-motivated and often preoccupied with their own material advancement. Authoritative and intelligent, they have the potential to make great leaders. The Fire Ox is a compassionate person and his or her actions are always fundamentally well-intentioned, but this Ox enjoys a sense of power and can become overbearing.

Fire Oxen are quick to react to people and circumstances; but unchecked, this instinctive, impetuous nature may alienate others, who could feel somewhat scorched by the Fire Oxen's knee-jerk, often harsh, responses. An inability to sit back and consider a situation also means that Fire Oxen may lose out on potential

THE OX 牛

opportunities, which is a pity as they particularly seek to champion good causes. Adversaries should take care, for these potential warriors have a temper that can easily turn combative – Fire Oxen will want to lead the first charge. All Fire Oxen would do well to consider before charging, however, as they may have a tendency to think rather more highly of themselves than reality warrants.

Fire Oxen should try to moderate the internal furnace by admitting their limitations, avoiding extremes and taking a steadier, step-by-step approach to building success. Paradoxically, only then can they be at their most powerful.

EARTH OX: 1949, 2009
"Ox in the Byre"

Being born in an Earth year provides a double helping of Earth characteristics for the already grounded Ox, concentrating the animal's hardworking nature. However, unlike the others of the Ox clan, the Earth Ox is usually aware of the limitations that such tenacity can bring. In keeping with timeless oriental ideals, the Earth Ox is refreshingly able to be satisfied with his or her circumstances.

Despite a strong sense of purpose, the Earth Ox is patient and contemplative, happy to live in the here and now, achieving life's important objectives slowly but surely. Earth Oxen plough on through difficulties or repetitive tasks without complaining. Honest and straightforward, they can be relied upon to show loyalty and integrity. Earth Oxen are sensible, practical and realistic, and capable of making good judgments about people and situations. At the same time, they can be as obstinate as any Ox. As this kind of Ox can lack a spirit of innovation, he or she is well advised to try to moderate the heightened Ox tendency for circumspection and love of routine in order not to miss out on important opportunities.

Not overly emotional but utterly sincere, these folks have a pleasant and nurturing way with others. They're affectionate and particularly loving with partners and family members. In the interests of digestive health (the digestive system is the organ system of the Earth Element), Earth Oxen would be wise to moderate their food intake, especially when it comes to rich, indulgent foods.

WORK, CAREER AND MONEY
Reliable; Honest; Single-minded; Logical; Determined

THE OX IN WORK AND CAREER

The Ox is one Chinese horoscope sign for which our stereotypical notions about the character of the agricultural ox or buffalo are actually reasonably accurate. Oxen may achieve career success by steady plodding. Metaphorically speaking, they plough a straight furrow – they finish one task before they even think about starting the next. They're perfectly happy with routine and a fixed schedule or structure – in fact, routine makes them feel secure. They're extremely comfortable in a hierarchical organization, provided they're reassured it has been solidly set up and is run on good foundations.

Oxen like to know their place and what's expected of them. They're extremely serious about their work; they like to think tasks through and plan carefully. They have tremendous organizational skills and pay meticulous attention to detail, assets they can apply to a very wide range of jobs and career options. Being associated with the fixed Element of Earth and being so naturally grounded, they're often drawn to work that involves the land, outdoors or buildings.

Oxen do not necessarily make the best team players. Although they're happy to be part of an organization, they prefer to have exclusive responsibility for their own area of work. They can be good managers, who treat their staff well, but they

---

COMMON CAREER POSSIBILITIES

• FARMING • GARDENING • HORTICULTURE • TEACHING
• REAL ESTATE AGENT • BANKER • ARCHITECT • POLICEMAN • SOLDIER
• MECHANIC • ENGINEER • DRAFTSMAN • TEACHER • COOK

have high expectations of their employees, calling upon them to work in exactly the same way they do themselves. Likeable, and utterly reliable, honest and trustworthy, Oxen will often work their way up to positions of authority and responsibility. They're also effective when in self-employment.

Above all, Oxen genuinely enjoy working as an activity in itself. In fact, many Oxen seem more at ease while working than at almost any other times in their lives; and they don't generally relish retirement.

THE OX AND MONEY

Oxen display the same range of qualities in their relationship with money as they do with work, business and career. Naturally honest and straightforward in their financial dealings, they can be utterly relied upon when handling other people's cash. Equally, they're methodical and highly organized about their own financial affairs. No Ox would want to consider relying upon anyone else to provide them with money – and equally they would expect others to have the same values and work ethic themselves, never asking for financial help. Conservative and traditional, they love mottoes and sayings: "Neither a borrower nor a lender be" is one that suits their attitude to money perfectly.

Oxen are concerned with financial security, and highly averse to risk. They would rather run a business based on modest but completely dependable sources of income and returns than gamble on big profits, and so run the risk of loss. Oxen have no enthusiasm for any kind of pecuniary drama. Nevertheless, in Chinese tradition, Oxen have a reputation for being able steadily to gather material assets. Step by step, year after year, they have the potential to build up great commercial empires. They'll put any gains to sensible use, probably reinvesting them wisely or saving them for the future – Oxen are not spendthrifts.

Oxen are also renowned for being meticulous – even fanatical – about settling their debts. They hate to owe people money, becoming troubled and embarrassed if they don't pay it back promptly. Finally, Oxen definitely don't believe in a "free lunch" – in their world, only hard work brings returns, and they're probably absolutely right to believe this.

PREFERENCES AND WELL-BEING
Proving stable in a storm

PEOPLE, TASTES AND PASTIMES

Those born in the year of the Ox tend to be conservative and somewhat old-fashioned in the way they view their relationships. With fixed ways to do things, they may seem uncompromising, which can frustrate those around them.

Introverted and cautious, Oxen tend not to have a huge social circle, but may nurture a smaller number of strong, trusted and lasting friendships that they build up over a long period of time. If you have an Ox as your friend, you're lucky indeed – his or her loyalty is unflinching and your friend will be the first on hand if you're in need. Oxen are not good at small talk, living by the principle that actions speak louder than words. He or she may not pick up the phone, but you may find a food parcel or other offer of help at your door if you need it.

Peaceful and calm, Oxen seek to live a quiet life, avoiding upset as much as possible. However, if trouble occurs or if their pride is hurt, they can be sulkers, carrying a grievance for a very long time. And if one of their occasional but famous temper attacks fires off, they can be extremely destructive – just like the idiomatic "bull in a china shop".

Oxen are certainly not the world's greatest hedonists. They prefer simplicity in their lifestyle and surroundings and show a strong tendency toward becoming addicted to their work. The Ox's simply laid-out home is an important place of peace, comfort, security and privacy, preferably shared with a devoted partner in a stable and long-term relationship. This need for stability means that Oxen also prefer to vacation close to home, perhaps venturing into the countryside to enjoy the wide-open spaces loved by the animals after whom they're named.

At home they like tasks that fully absorb them, such as gardening, cooking or crafts, taking pleasure in aiming for perfection through intricate steps and attention to detail. They want to create something valuable or beautiful, or both.

HEALTH AND WELL-BEING
Fixed Element: Earth

The Ox clan is known for its inherent constitutional strength, endurance and ability to withstand the onslaughts of time and life's challenges – as in the saying, "as strong as an ox". In the East, those born under the sign of the Ox are reputed to enjoy the longest lives. However, the Ox's strengths can also lead to eaknesses, meaning that, as always, balance is key.

Oxen thrive in rural settings, preferring the open spaces of the countryside to an intense city milieu. However, the greatest threat to the Ox's well-being, wherever he or she lives and works, is his or her tendency to work too hard for too long. Oxen often need to be reminded to take a break, including a vacation.

Oxen are not generally anxious types, but can suffer if they are too emotionally restrained, bottling things up before potentially exploding. Threats to self-sufficiency – perhaps by having to bend to the will of others – are the one thing that the Ox finds particularly stressful, damaging fundamental Ox pride. If the Ox does become upset, however, he or she is unlikely to want to talk about it, instead preferring to further immerse him- or herself in work. However, this really only exacerbates the problem, potentially leading to general ill-health.

Oxen tend to be sedentary in their work and way of life. This can cause problems with the legs, knees and other joints, possibly leading to arthritis or related problems. For these reasons, Ox people should make a conscious effort to get up and move about during the day and to take regular exercise.

The Earth Element is associated with the organ system of the stomach, spleen and pancreas and so with digestive and weight issues. The Ox is a natural grazer, and has a weakness for eating lots of heavy, rich, fatty or acidic foods. He or she also shows a tendency to eat a limited variety of foods. Altogether these factors can wreak havoc with digestion and cause weight gain, especially considering the general levels of inactivity associated with the Ox. As well as regular exercise, a healthy, varied diet is essential for Oxen, who should also remember that their love of order and regime often makes dieting successful – even enjoyable – for them.

THE TWELVE ANIMAL SIGNS | 虎

THE TIGER

TIGER YEARS: 1902, 1914, 1926, 1938, 1950, 1962, 1974, 1986, 1998, 2010, 2022, 2034
TIGER HOURS: 0300–0500
FIXED ELEMENT: WOOD   **YANG SIGN**

The Tiger person wants to be wild and free, and constantly strives to do extraordinary things. He or she is courageous and undaunted by risk, and impossible to tame. Tigers love to stand out: they express dramatic emotion and cannot live without attention. They're always ready to be the hero, to adopt a new cause, to fight against an injustice or to beat a pathway into hostile territory.

Powerful and passionate, persuasive and charming, the Tiger has lots of personal magnetism. Yet this big cat has another side to its nature, for there is quite a lot of "front" going on here. Although socially adept, the Tiger can be a loner, too, and is often hard to get to know properly. Behind the brash exterior, Tigers can be emotionally low at times, possibly even descending into despair or gloom. During such times of unhappiness, Tigers need the enduring comfort and support of those who are nearest to them to restore their emotional well-being. Tigers are always unpredictable or changeable, and often foolish, ignoring conventional wisdom or advice. However, their indomitable spirit and determination to succeed always enable them to bounce back in the end. Indeed, the Tiger has that feline knack of nearly always landing on his or her feet.

The Tiger's complementary and opposite sign is the Rabbit.

KEYWORDS
• POWERFUL • PASSIONATE • ROMANTIC • DYNAMIC • DARING
• ADVENTUROUS • MAGNETIC • EGOTISTIC • FIERY • BOLD • CHARISMATIC
• INDEPENDENT • UNPREDICTABLE • RESTLESS • RECKLESS • IMPULSIVE

THE TWELVE ANIMAL SIGNS

THE FIVE TYPES OF TIGER

METAL TIGER: 1950, 2010
"Tiger Leaving the Mountain"
Determined, focused and at times aggressive, the Metal Tiger can be ambitious and single-minded in pursuit of a goal. Despite an underlying set of clearly honed principles and a defining altruism, the Metal Tiger is likely to be candid and perhaps even undiplomatic – and he or she always knows best.

The self-confident Metal type is particularly active in the Tiger, creating a hard worker who is good at planning, decision-making, engaging others, and getting things done. As long as his or her employees are not too sensitive – the Metal Tiger speaks his or her mind and can be moody and inflexible – this is a decisive leader, who can think and act quickly and lead from the front.

This Tiger tends to be all about "me". He or she will sweep up the fruits of their hard labour, accumulating them for the benefit of the self, rather than others. Justifiably, the Metal Tiger is said to make a good friend, but a formidable enemy – this is definitely a personality to keep on your side. Passionate and uncompromising, the Metal Tiger will look for similar attributes in his or her partner, but for smooth relationships (at work, as well as at home), he or she would do well to try to become more flexible, and more diplomatic. Health is less often an issue for Metal Tigers, whose strong lungs, the organ system of the Metal Element, provide them with powerful, energizing breath.

WATER TIGER: 1902, 1962, 2022
"Tiger Passing through the Forest"
A typically restless animal, the Tiger is calmed by the Water Element. Water beautifully balances many of the Tiger's more striking and aggressive traits, creating the most intuitive, empathetic and perceptive of all the Tiger types.

A more conciliatory beast than other Tigers, the Water Tiger may be direct, but is also more able to listen to, engage with and understand the thoughts and feelings of others. The results are fewer unnecessary fights and a greater ability to assess situations with an open mind, making the Water Tiger's conclusions more accurate and reliable than others in the clan. The Water Tiger has a strong interest in fighting for good causes and can approach problems with a host of fresh ideas and plenty of intuition. This animal has a greater sense of insight than other Tiger types, which makes him or her better at taking the longer-term view. Home life and family are also more important than with the other Tigers.

However, this Tiger's ability to be more thoughtful can also make him or her considerably less decisive. When the feelings of others come into consideration, the Water Tiger can become less certain of his or her overall direction, and so prone to procrastination, preferring rather too easily to go with the flow.

The kidneys and urinary system are the organs associated with Water, which can become depleted through stress. In order to maintain his or her balance of *chi* energy, the Water Tiger should beware of overdoing things for too long, striking a carefully controlled work–life balance.

WOOD TIGER: 1914, 1974, 2034
"Tiger Holding Still"

Wood is the fixed Element for the Tiger, so this Tiger type has a double helping of Wood energy. The result is a somewhat softer type of Tiger, demonstrating qualities of stability, rootedness, imagination and artistic creativity.

This Tiger type is generally less fierce, confrontational, daunting and inscrutable than the other tigers. As a result, this Tiger is a better team player, with a warmer nature. He or she will tend to be adaptable, popular and generous, and place a particular importance on friendship. Despite his or her inherent single-mindedness and dislike of being told what to do, this Tiger soon learns that popularity can also bring success. Observant and imaginative, the Wood Tiger can build a strong, loyal team that is willing to work hard for its leader's own benefit. His or her cautious feline nature ensures that this Tiger weighs up the

THE TWELVE ANIMAL SIGNS

options before taking a lithe leap into action. The result can be a successful businessperson with the potential for great accumulated wealth.

Contrary to the general Tiger loathing for being tied down – which might express itself in the Wood Tiger's fickle attitude to work – this Tiger places emphasis on having a stable family and home life. However, the Wood Tiger is also prone to strong emotions and lack of self-control, so he or she might have a temper that's best kept in check. Wood Tigers would be wise to limit their alcohol intake, which can exacerbate proneness to rage, and also weaken *chi* flowing through the liver and gall bladder, the organ system of Wood.

FIRE TIGER: 1926, 1986
"Tiger in the Forest"

The Fire type is probably the most extreme Tiger, bringing trailblazing, explosive energy and powerful action, as well as capacity for dynamic communication, influence and expression.

With typical characteristics of drama, passion, excitement, enthusiasm, liveliness and abundant energy, the Fire Tiger can make a forceful leader, who is always ready to speak up and take charge, persuading others to his or her way of thinking and enthusing them about his or her ideas. Sincere and principled, this Tiger may be intolerant of those who take an opposing view, or who are overly cautious, and may lack the empathy evident in the Wood and Water types.

Signs of animal nature are rife in the Fire Tiger. Predatory, determined and quick, this Tiger has an overarching need for freedom, and can become quickly restless. This big cat lives in the moment, pouncing on opportunity – sometimes recklessly – while also eagerly sniffing out the next adventure. If you live with a Fire Tiger be prepared for a life that is dramatic, impulsive and unpredictable.

The Fire Tiger's impetuous and unconventional nature, and dislike for taking on board the counsel of others, leads to many ups and downs in emotions and fortunes. There are no half-measures with this Tiger – both mistakes and successes tend to be big ones. However, his or her own irrepressible optimism and generous spirit have strong effects on other people, perhaps overwhelmingly so.

The Fire Tiger lacks moderation, so he or she may quickly overindulge – in terms of food and drink and in terms of commitment to work and others. The result is both physical and mental stress, which can take its toll on the Tiger's health – especially of the heart and circulation, the organ system of Fire.

EARTH TIGER: 1938, 1998
"Tiger Crossing the Mountain"

The Earth Element creates a Tiger that is more grounded and centred than other Tigers, with more practicality and common sense, and greater powers of concentration. Reasonable and sensible, realistic and wise, observant and focused, Earth Tigers take a nurturing approach to the world. They're relatively quiet and compassionate creatures, who are concerned for the needs of others, and they often adopt humanitarian causes in their work or hobbies.

The least restless of the Tiger clan, Earth Tigers are probably also the least pioneering and adventurous. These are cats who care what others think of them and may take advice in order to preserve their reputations. With their patient, serious and responsible natures, they take a methodical approach to success, preferring to keep things under their own control in order to minimize the worry to which they're prone. Their innate staying power means they can use persistent effort to resolve problems.

All Tigers are innately good at handling risk, which makes the Earth Tiger's aversion to the unpredictable something of a contradiction in terms. In order to counteract their anxiety and move forward, Earth Tigers should try not to ponder too long before taking action, advancing steadily and calmly at a pace with which they feel comfortable.

The organs associated with the Earth Element are the spleen, stomach and pancreas, which makes weight gain a weak spot for Earth Tigers. In addition, worry can exacerbate stomach problems, so the Earth Tiger should try to moderate his or her intake of sugar and fatty foods and minimize exposure to stress, keeping in mind the bigger picture and long-term outcomes, rather than getting stuck in the detail.

WORK, CAREER AND MONEY
Creative; Leader; Adventurous; Speculator; Spendthrift

THE TIGER IN WORK AND CAREER
A notoriously quick thinker, the Tiger can deftly master tasks and acquire skills. Coupled with the Tiger's love of a challenge and change, this means that this person is well advised to find a job to provide plenty of excitement and variety – or to change his or her occupation or career relatively frequently. Tigers like to be on the cutting edge, pushing the boundaries and venturing into the unknown, like some sort of 19th-century explorer transposed into the modern world.

A job that is too repetitive, structured or restrained can send the Tiger on the prowl, casting his or her eye into the jungle to find some new challenge. Danger and hardship are no turn-off – the Tiger relishes the opportunity to sharpen his or her claws and display a remarkable capacity to fight and to win. Tigers might growl in despair if things don't work out – but they're perfectly happy to start all over again. However, knee-jerk reactions can lead to reckless decision-making and Tiger people may do well to force themselves to stop and think. Nevertheless, Tigers constantly drive forward, determined to succeed.

Tigers enjoy taking the initiative and exerting influence over others. They prove themselves, time and again, to be inspirational leaders with a direct – albeit sometimes undiplomatic – leadership style. They also have a genuine wish to help those who work with and for them, sometimes in unexpected ways.

COMMON CAREER POSSIBILITIES
• ADVERTISING • PUBLICITY • TRAVEL • DRIVING • TOURING
• SALES • SPORTS • POLICE • ARMED FORCES • PERFORMING ARTS
• POLITICS • BUSINESS • MANAGEMENT • TEACHING

THE TIGER 虎

Expect to find a Tiger among the executives and other big players in an organization, providing the creative initiative, the drive for success and the inspiration for change. However, beware if a Tiger is in charge of a budget. This is a risk-taker, who may play fast and loose with someone else's resources. The Tiger is happiest starting from scratch, determining how the game works, and then perhaps moving on. For this reason, Tigers make great entrepreneurs, but they don't always have the organizational skills or patience for the mundane tasks – such as book-keeping and administration – that self-employment requires.

THE TIGER AND MONEY

Tigers love power – and that means they also love money, especially spending it. In an ideal world a Tiger will fill his or her closet with designer labels, the best clothes that money can buy. The Tiger's home brims with lovely things and he or she will want to take exotic or expensive holidays. Luckily for them, Tigers seem to be financially fortunate. With their unfailing belief that everything will work out in the end, they're happy to take financial risks and – like the cats they are – will tend to land on their feet. Although the Tiger might experience considerable ups and downs in their fortunes, through hard work and creativity they know they can generate more where that came from – easy come, easy go. As long as they're in charge of their own financial fortunes, that is. With their deep-seated need to be in control and have freedom to do as they wish, Tigers are unlikely to let anyone else make financial decisions for them.

Tigers make great speculators, willing to take risks and keen to keep going until they see a turnaround in their fortunes. Innovative investments are what attract the Tiger – he or she would never want to play things safe. Even where money is concerned, the Tiger is attracted to the heady adventure of risk-taking. However, Tigers have a tendency to move their financial investments on too quickly, taking the hit on short-term losses rather than waiting for long-term gains. But that probably wouldn't worry them too much.

Despite their self-centred natures, Tigers are generous with their money and spread the financial benefit around.

THE TWELVE ANIMAL SIGNS

PREFERENCES AND WELL-BEING
Pursuing action and adventure

PEOPLE, TASTES AND PASTIMES
The Tiger tends to live a life of high intensity – a roller coaster of ups and downs, swift changes of direction and surprises around every corner. If there's ever a danger of a dull moment, the Tiger will want to do something about it. Those in a relationship with a Tiger should hold on tight for the ride – if they do, they'll be rewarded through the Tiger's boundless generosity, willingness to help and unwavering positivity that can raise the spirits of everyone around them. Never try to tame the Tiger, however, as this animal likes freedom of choice and is liable to change his or her mind. He or she wants to be in charge, refusing to listen to the advice of others. The Tiger can also be obstinate and uncompromising in his or her relationships, which can make for friendships that require a great deal of leniency, forgiveness and understanding on the part of the friend. Finally, beware of crossing a Tiger – these people do not appreciate being slighted and can take offence easily, sometimes to the point of wanting revenge.

Unconventional and experimental, the Tiger wants to exercise freedom of expression in the way he or she looks. Fashion-conscious with creative flair, the Tiger is a naturally sharp dresser and has expensive tastes in clothes, and also in decor. At home Tigers like to be surrounded by beautiful things that embody their need for self-expression. Expect to find exotic objects acquired on their travels, or aspirational objects that remind them of the places they want to go.

Travel and exploration is a recurring theme for the adventurous Tiger, who may spontaneously take a trip to find new, exciting and dramatic experiences. Back at home, the Tiger is a party animal, relishing being the centre of attention on the social scene. Favourite hobbies tend to involve high levels of activity and adventure. Tigers love extreme sports (such as motor racing, which indulges the Tiger's love of driving, too) and are often the first to sign up to the current fad –

in fact, they're probably the ones to start a fad themselves. Natural show-offs, Tigers may be drawn to activities that involve performing, such as local drama, dance or music groups.

HEALTH AND WELL-BEING
Fixed Element: Wood

The Wood Element is associated with the season of spring with its life-giving energy and vitality. It's hardly surprising, then, that Tigers exhibit constant bursts of energy that mean they travel through life at full steam, constantly seeking new experiences and challenges. With all that raw vitality coursing through their veins, Tigers have an enviable ability to bounce back, quickly recovering from tiredness or even illness. However, after many years of living on the roller coaster, Tigers are at serious risk of exhaustion.

To achieve greater balance and avoid burning out, Tigers may be well advised to take steps to avoid extremes as much as possible. They can take time for adventure, but also make time for rest – Tigers can be quite good at becoming fully absorbed in a quiet activity if they find something that interests them. They may also benefit from considering the risks when indulging in dangerous activities – inevitably accidents and incidents will happen if they don't take care.

The organs associated with the Wood Element are the liver and gall bladder, which means that Tigers should avoid overindulgence (particularly of rich, creamy foods and of alcohol), and eat plenty of leafy green vegetables and sprouting plants, which are themselves governed by the Wood Element and will keep these organs healthy.

Psychologically, Tigers are prone to feeling dejected at times – and although these fiercely independent creatures may not immediately admit it, what they really need is reassuring and unconditional love and support from those around them. Buoyed up by this love, the Tiger soon returns to "normality". Feeling caged in for a prolonged period can produce some of the worst problems for the Tiger. Getting out into nature is the answer, in order to reconnect with the influences of the Wood Element and set the Tiger's adventurous spirit free.

THE RABBIT

RABBIT YEARS: 1903, 1915, 1927, 1939, 1951, 1963, 1975, 1987, 1999, 2011, 2023
RABBIT HOURS: 0500–0700
FIXED ELEMENT: WOOD   YIN SIGN

The humble Rabbit person eschews standing out in a crowd. Unfortunately, this can give the impression of aloofness, but nothing could be further from the truth. Rabbits are generally timid creatures, who overwhelmingly need security in order to reach their significant potential in life. They'll always take the path of least resistance, maintaining harmony in order to move forward. To this end, they'll go a long way to avoid confrontation and aggression, often keeping their opinions to themselves in order not to upset the status quo. Such risk aversion can mean they miss out on important opportunities, and those around them may view them as indecisive or weak.

However, within their comfort zone, Rabbits have a strong will to pursue their objectives. Compassionate, diplomatic and benign, they make great negotiators. Their strong sense of self-preservation can make them quietly manipulative. They're extremely thorough, often to the point of fussiness, and excellent at recovering from calamities – Rabbits are the ultimate survivors. Thanks to their generous natures and the way they accommodate, empathize with and support others, Rabbits are popular, with the potential for great contentment.

The Rabbit's complementary and opposite sign is the Tiger.

KEYWORDS
• PRIVATE • DIPLOMATIC • CULTURED • INSCRUTABLE
• WELL-MANNERED • GENTLE • CARING • SENSITIVE • PLAYFUL • PRIVATE
• ARTISTIC • STYLISH • TIMID • SENTIMENTAL • RESERVED • CUNNING

THE FIVE TYPES OF RABBIT

METAL RABBIT: 1951, 2011
"Rabbit in the Burrow"
The Metal Element produces a sharper, more dynamic and more decisive type of Rabbit, who pursues his or her goals with greater tenacity. With his or her considerable strength of character, and deeper emotional intensity than most of the other Rabbits, the Metal Rabbit is generally more robust in mind and body.

Metal Rabbits are happier than others in the role of leader. They immerse themselves in their work, are confident when dealing with others, and are less willing to compromise than other Rabbits. Fully committed, they toil for long hours and are sensitive to what's going on around them. They're also more willing to come out from the shadows and take responsibility than other Rabbit types.

The Rabbit's good intuition is accompanied in Metal Rabbits by an extra helping of animal cunning that may not always be obvious to those around them. On the other hand, Metal Rabbits can usually see through others' attempts at deceit and are more likely to expose it than others in their clan.

Metal Rabbits can be prone to "creative block" and may be taken over by worry. Safe surroundings filled with a few, well-known and trusted people is the perfect antidote to this, helping to coax Metal Rabbits out of their anxiety and so protecting the health of the lungs and large intestine, the organ system of Metal.

WATER RABBIT: 1903, 1963, 2023
"Rabbit Running in the Forest"
The Water Element emphasizes the Rabbit's placid nature. Reflective, intuitive and flexible, this Rabbit is acutely attuned to his or her own feelings and sensitive toward the feelings of others. Acute powers of intuition and empathy can make Water Rabbits appear almost psychic in their ability to tap into what's on

someone's mind. Sympathetic and tolerant, Water Rabbits are great listeners who easily understand other points of view, and willingly give counsel and support, although they may also be too easily influenced. Overall, the Water Rabbit is well liked, and is rewarded for his or her own sensitivity with the sensitivity of others.

However, such gentleness is not without its shortcomings. Water Rabbits can be timid and their emotions can be delicate. Strongly affected by events going on around them, Water Rabbits, more than any other kind, need to avoid conflict or confrontation. In their own lives, they're inclined to hesitancy or indecision and they may become obsessed by negative experiences, turning them over in their minds. Water Rabbits, therefore, can be overly cautious or suspicious.

All the same, Water Rabbits are chatty people who generally get on well with others and have deeply romantic natures. They may appear self-absorbed, but that's not really what's going on – they're probably just thinking things over.

Overall, Water Rabbits are well advised not to let others take advantage of them, balancing their willingness to trust with some of their innate caution. In this way they can keep a healthy balance of *chi* in their kidneys and bladder, the organ system of Water. They should try not to give in too easily before thinking of their own feelings – a little less flexibility can be a good thing. Finding love with a more powerful animal sign, such as the Tiger, can help the Water Rabbit come out from the safety of the burrow to leap forward and have a good time!

WOOD RABBIT: 1915, 1975
"Enlightened Rabbit"

The double helping of the Wood Element in this type of Rabbit makes him or her an especially nurturing and imaginative person. Wood Rabbits are compassionate to a fault, and desperate to avoid hurting or offending others, but this can make them wary of commitment. Keen on justice, they possess an extra dose of the Rabbit's peace-loving nature. They have their own ambitions, but can be easily put off pursuing them, because they don't like to make a fuss and simply want to fit in. They can often find themselves putting other people's priorities ahead of their own.

Sociable and gregarious, Wood Rabbits enjoy others' company and love to be constantly busy, especially in collaborative effort. They should, though, make sure they get enough rest, as they are prone to worry if they take on too much.

Woodland creatures through and through, Wood Rabbits have a deep affinity with aesthetic beauty and the natural world. These are particularly creative people, who are often good at art and will draw upon a wide range of experiences for their inspiration. But they also fare well in business, moving upward through a large organization with steady success.

In general, Wood Rabbits should try to speak up for themselves forcefully, drawing on some of the metaphorical bile in the liver and gall bladder, the organ system of Wood. Reticence to choose a stance and stick with it can cause others to lose respect, so activities that inspire inner confidence – quiet pastimes such as meditation or physical character-building activities such as sports – are all good options for the Wood Rabbit.

FIRE RABBIT: 1927, 1987
"Rabbit Dreaming of the Moon"

This Rabbit type is more dynamic and intense, active and decisive, and bolder and less conventional than others in its clan. Altogether, this Rabbit has the makings of a very successful combination of characteristics.

Fire Rabbits love fun, adventure and travel. They're pursuers of happiness, for themselves and for others, and they're less concerned with material or financial objects than other animal signs. They're more likely than other Rabbits to take some risks and perhaps even set aside their scruples once in a while.

Fire Rabbits, like all Rabbits, are intuitive and sensitive, but Fire Rabbits are particularly charming, able to woo others with their words. They're influential leaders, who may use their charm to disguise their wishes, preferring subterfuge to open conflict. If things don't go their way, they should avoid dwelling on the setbacks and instead attract others' support to help them re-light their inner fire.

Although basically they want a quiet life, Fire Rabbits are more emotionally volatile than other types. They have a bit of a temper, and are more likely to express themselves angrily when they feel hurt – which is not necessarily a bad thing. When threatened, they can even become aggressive toward other people. They should try to moderate their anger, though, in order not to place strain on their heart and circulation, the organ system of the Fire Element.

As partners, Fire Rabbits are affectionate and adventurous, although they would do well to keep in check their propensity for mood swings.

EARTH RABBIT: 1939, 1999
"Rabbit Running out of the Forest"

The Earth Element brings quiet, calm, steady practicality and worldly materialism to the Rabbit archetype, creating a personality rich with common sense. The Earth Rabbit is a considered thinker, who can make balanced, shrewd decisions.

Brilliantly organized and persistently hardworking, Earth Rabbits can be capable, entrepreneurial people, who set realistic objectives. They'll steadily climb the ladder of success, often in a calculated way, as these Rabbits are more preoccupied with self-advancement than other types. Their carefulness can make them overly fussy, but it also makes them good at accumulating wealth.

Although Earth Rabbits are less likely to accommodate the needs of others than other Rabbit types, the typical Earth qualities of kindliness and nurturing mean they're also renowned for doing good for others. For this reason, they tend to be highly respected individuals.

Despite showing great confidence and competence at work, Earth Rabbits need secure homes that offer retreat from the outside world. They look for steady, dependable relationships. However, to reach their full potential, Earth Rabbits should try to resist any temptation to hide from the world, particularly when they're under pressure. Inclined to deep introspection during times of crisis, they should avoid taking on too much in all areas of their lives to minimize the opportunities for worry. Regular exercise will help restore confidence, and also help combat the tendency toward weight gain – which may occur when there is an imbalance of fundamental *chi* energy in the stomach, spleen and pancreas, the organ system of the Earth Element.

THE TWELVE ANIMAL SIGNS

WORK, CAREER AND MONEY
Diligence; Diplomacy; Organization; Cunning

THE RABBIT IN WORK AND CAREER

Rabbits are sharp and intelligent, imaginative and creative, quietly gathering all the facts and thinking things through before making judgments and taking action. This makes them highly reliable employees and business partners. They have excellent organizational skills, and they're adaptable – as long as they don't have to behave in a way that makes them feel uncomfortable.

Skillful communicators, Rabbits have a wide repertoire of interpersonal skills. They're persuasive, diplomatic and empathetic, which makes them great at negotiation. However, they can dislike being the leader, feeling most at home as one of the key cogs in the wheel. That's not to say that Rabbits are not ambitious – they're often celebrated for their ability to rise through the ranks of their chosen career by a careful combination of application, likeability and shrewd strategy (they know exactly what to say when and to whom). Popular among their colleagues, Rabbits are appreciated for their ability to ease the operating systems within an organization. They're comfortable with self-employment, as they enjoy working at their own speed, and they make especially great business partners, particularly when paired with a more dynamic sign, such as the Tiger.

However, never ask a Rabbit to get involved in work conflicts. The more pressurized or cut-throat side of business is likely to be too stressful for Rabbits.

COMMON CAREER POSSIBILITIES

• THERAPY • COUNSELLING • BEAUTY • DIPLOMATIC SERVICE
• FASHION BUYER • PR REPRESENTATIVE • CAMPAIGNER • ARTIST • LAWYER
• CHURCH ADMINISTRATOR • WRITER • TEACHER • DESIGNER • NEGOTIATOR

They also become anxious around disorganized working practices, or a messy working environment – although they can quite happily sort out the mess as part of their job and then keep things tidily ticking over.

THE RABBIT AND MONEY

In Chinese astrology, the Rabbit has a reputation for being financially fortunate – but in Chinese terms luck is not the same as chance. Rather, it's the result of the application of particular qualities and skills.

Rabbits don't accumulate wealth through playing power games and taking risks. As is more in keeping with their nature, they have more subtle ways of working. On the face of it, Rabbits may appear to many people to be a bit slow and not terribly bright, but in fact, when it comes to matters of finance, they have an acute nose for a good deal. They show careful, even meticulous attention to detail, always checking the fine print before committing to any transaction. Tactical operators, they're notoriously good at weighing up people and situations, and they make many friendships that can be of help to them. As a result of their ability to hide what they're really thinking, Rabbits can make excellent negotiators. Others can find it very difficult to know what a Rabbit might be willing to concede. With their outwardly mild manners, Rabbits are able to be unobtrusively ruthless in the pursuit of their objectives. Furthermore, they're experts at self-preservation – and not at all above a bit of double dealing.

Rabbits hate financial disorder – whether in their own affairs, the affairs of others or in the economy at large. However, because they're great survivors and great organizers, they'll tend to put in place as many financial safety nets as possible and these, along with their shrewdness and flexibility, will enable them to weather the worst of financial storms without any drama. Rabbits are the people to survive harsh economic times that might see other signs in financial crisis.

When it comes to spending money, Rabbits splash out on their homes. They prefer to invest in art or antiques rather than risk their cash on the stock market, so they fill their homes with beautiful treasures, as well as high-quality clothing, and fine food and wines – all essentials for their discerning tastes.

THE TWELVE ANIMAL SIGNS

PREFERENCES AND WELL-BEING
Finding stability and harmony

PEOPLE, TASTES AND PASTIMES

Rabbit people seek out positive, stable relationships with other people that are based on harmony and compromise – and they can't see why others don't always do the same, becoming embarrassed if anyone makes any trouble. Rabbits are extremely sociable – they happily join groups and societies – and have a quiet sense of humour. Sympathetic and helpful, these gentle people make wonderful friends, renowned for their listening skills and their ability to give good advice.

Rabbits are deeply interested in style, culture and the arts. They're highly sophisticated individuals who pay a lot of attention to fashion and the latest trends, and they love to dress in clothes of the finest quality. As Rabbits are sedate characters, who prefer to blend in, their style is understated elegance and unlikely to be in the least bit showy or brash. Don't expect a Rabbit to overlook style *faux pas* in others – they can be extremely snobbish!

Rabbits look for serene and harmonious experiences when they relax. On vacation they travel to places that indulge their interest in aesthetics and high culture – you might expect to find them in cities such as Rome, Florence or Paris, which have strong links with the arts. When they aren't in a gallery, they'll be searching through boutiques to find treasures to bring home as mementoes.

At home, you might find them nose-deep in their favourite novel, or enjoying great food and wine in a top-end restaurant – that's when they're not simply relaxing and chatting with their friends. Rabbits are likely to take courses in such subjects as painting, dance or music to indulge their love of the arts.

A Rabbit's home needs to be comfortable, secure and safe. Tasteful and stylish ornaments satisfy the Rabbit's need to be surrounded by culture, but an equally strong need for order means that every item is carefully chosen and no surface is overloaded with clutter. Rabbits simply cannot tolerate a mess.

THE RABBIT

HEALTH AND WELL-BEING
Fixed Element: Wood

Despite being known for having a particularly delicate constitution and being prone to nervousness and over-sensitivity, Rabbits tend to be among the longest-lived of the animal signs. Nevertheless, they're indeed prone to emotional stress, and they often demonstrate psychosomatic tendencies.

What is the key to this paradox? Chinese medicine sees health as determined by two things – constitutional health from birth, and the way in which we live. On the whole, Rabbits are particularly self-disciplined people, who tend to live in keeping with their constitutional characteristics – and if they don't, they suffer, learn from their mistakes and mend their ways to restore health. Being aware of their vulnerability makes Rabbits the world's greatest survivors.

Rabbits experience high levels of stress if they're exposed to the things they don't like: bad behaviour, poor or untidy working conditions, pressure to meet deadlines or speak publicly, having to take risks, and lack of creative stimulation can all be extremely stressful situations for the Rabbit. Stress might manifest itself as a digestive disorder, or simply send the Rabbit hopping quickly into his or her burrow to hide. However, as long as Rabbits resist the tendency to become addicted to work, they're generally adept at avoiding stressful situations. Even if they can't steer clear of them altogether, they're brilliant at stepping back and taking time out to rest and recover quickly once the pressure is off. In doing so, they restore their physical and mental health.

However, the Rabbits' love of the good things in life – good food, good wine, and social gatherings that might last late into the night – coupled with their need for comfort and relaxing at home mean they can easily fall into a lazy and indulgent lifestyle. The organ system associated with their fixed Element, Wood, is the liver, so all Rabbits would be well advised to make sure that, except for special occasions, they avoid alcohol and eat good-quality but simple food that is not too rich – and not too much of it. They should avoid staying up too late at night too often and take regular fresh air and exercise: the Rabbit who lives in the countryside and strides out for regular walks is the healthiest of all.

THE TWELVE ANIMAL SIGNS | 龍

THE DRAGON

DRAGON YEARS: 1904, 1916, 1928, 1940, 1952, 1964, 1976, 1988, 2000, 2012, 2024
DRAGON HOURS: 0700–0900
FIXED ELEMENT: EARTH   YANG SIGN

In the West we think of the dragon as a horrific, fire-breathing monster. In Chinese lore, the dragon is a symbol of power and authority, but also of good fortune – although it is not also without its terrifying characteristics.

All Dragon types are highly confident and self-assured, refusing to conform and dominating those around them. Free spirits, untrammelled by the petty concerns of those they consider lesser mortals, Dragons may get carried away with their egos in the pursuit of their goals, eschewing rules and regulations and coming across as highly assertive, arrogant and intolerant.

Their unyielding self-belief means that most Dragons turn out to be high achievers who love attention and refuse to compromise or take orders. As leaders they demand the same high standards of those around them as they do of themselves. They aren't completely infallible, though – Dragons can be so straightforward as to be naïve on occasion, and their impatience and reluctance to accept help can put them at risk of burning out. On the plus side, when a Dragon champions a good cause, he or she is likely to give support generously – and to enlist the support of others.

The Dragon's complementary and opposite sign is the Snake.

KEYWORDS

• CHARISMATIC • FLAMBOYANT • ENERGETIC • HEROIC • AUTHORITATIVE
• POWERFUL • DECISIVE • FEARLESS • DETERMINED • RESOURCEFUL
• OPTIMISTIC • IMPULSIVE • IRREPRESSIBLE • TEMPERAMENTAL • PROUD

THE FIVE TYPES OF DRAGON

METAL DRAGON: 1940, 2000
"Dragon of Patience"

The most intense and dominant of the Dragon clan, the Metal Dragon is as inflexible as iron. Metal Dragons rarely doubt their abilities or the rightness of their views. They have a largely unshakeable can-do attitude, and will not endure fools. They're defiant, outspoken and critical, and may be lacking in sympathy and sensitivity, often subduing others in what they see as their rightful quest.

Action-oriented Metal Dragons are people who make things happen, turning every vision into reality. Fanatical in their pursuit of their goals, retreat is never an option. Passionate leaders, they enthuse and inspire their followers – and if no one will follow them, that's not a problem as Metal Dragons enjoy combat and will happily go it alone. However, this stand-alone spirit can leave them isolated – Metal Dragons rarely have many close friends. If you're friends with a Metal Dragon, though, you're well protected by a fearsome and unyielding ally, whom few will dare to cross.

Being single-minded does not necessarily mean being unfair, and Metal Dragons are among the most honest signs in the Chinese zodiac, with strong convictions and a deep sense of integrity. If they perceive something to be dangerous or evil, they'll happily work on behalf of others to overcome it.

These tough individuals can benefit greatly from being more flexible, diplomatic and conciliatory, and less demanding in the standards they require of themselves and especially of other people. Metal Dragons should learn to recognize that inner strength comes in many guises and that others may be strong, too – only in different ways. And it wouldn't do them any harm to lighten up and be a bit playful, once in a while – which will help ease the pressure on their lungs, the organ system of the Metal Element.

WATER DRAGON: 1952, 2012
"Rain Dragon"

Water combined with the fiery nature of the Dragon provides a calming influence for some of this sign's more extreme qualities. Deeper and more intuitive, and more thoughtful and reflective, this Dragon type is less egotistical and power-hungry than the others in its clan.

A cooler approach to judgment and decision-making, and greater open-mindedness, mean that this is a more tactful and sensitive Dragon type, who is willing to listen to the opinions of others and is more concerned with others' well-being. As a result, Water Dragons are relatively good team players, forming co-operative relationships that work for the common good. With fewer egotistical tendencies, greater patience and greater wisdom in the execution of their plans, Water Dragons are more likely to find that others buy into their ideas, and by encouraging greater collaborative effort, they can achieve greater success. They'll also tend to have a larger circle of friends than other Dragon types.

Like all Dragons, Water Dragons may display extremely fiery will and tend to be dynamic and undaunted individuals. Combined with the intelligence brought by the Water Element and its ability to flow around obstacles, this Dragon's fire can overcome any obstacle – by using brains as well as brawn.

The Water Dragon's weak spot is that he or she may try to do too much, spreading him- or herself too thinly. Water Dragons are well advised to try to prioritize the important projects in their lives, delegating – or relinquishing altogether – those that have lower priority. Greater focus on a few important projects will help to preserve the Water Dragon's *chi*, or fundamental energy, which resides in the kidneys, the organ system of the Water Element.

WOOD DRAGON: 1904, 1864, 2024
"Dragon at the Whirlpool"

The Dragon born under the influence of the Wood Element is a more creative, imaginative and artistic type, while at the same time retaining the down-to-earth qualities that the fixed Earth Element already endows. With their greater personal warmth and more reasonable nature, these Dragons might be thought of as something of a "middle way".

Open to ideas and input from others, Wood Dragons – amazingly for any Dragon – can tolerate other people questioning their views and may even put others' views into practice. In general, they're far less likely to ride roughshod over others in order to push their own ideas through. Wood Dragons are able to evaluate situations carefully – sometimes even analyzing too much, resulting in long and needless debate both in their heads and with others. Once they've reached their conclusions, Wood Dragons can be innovative and creative in the execution of their plans. Aware of their own shortcomings, these Dragons are more realistic than other Dragon types and are able to keep one eye on the risks involved in each of the options available to them. Without the blind self-confidence that's typical of other Dragon types, but retaining the Dragon's fundamental inner strength, they can achieve success through a combination of logical evaluation and gutsy self-belief. Their personable nature means that they're also more likely to have a team of people behind them to support their cause.

Nevertheless, even though they're generally more compromising, Wood Dragons can turn nasty when challenged. The Wood Element governs the liver and gall bladder, the seats of our emotions. In order to live a balanced life, the Wood Dragon is therefore well-advised take care to control his or her temper.

FIRE DRAGON: 1916, 1976
"Dragon Flying to Heaven"

The addition of the Fire Element to the already fiery Dragon produces the ultimate Dragon type: powerful, dynamic and forceful, passionate and full of explosive energy. This Dragon is fearless for himself, and fearsome to others.

Oozing extreme self-confidence and self-importance, Fire Dragons can be domineering in their interactions with other people. As a result they do not easily win allies or friends, often scaring people away. However, this Dragon type believes he or she does not need anyone else. The Fire Dragon is always poised to fight a challenge head on and alone – and will even seek out tests of strength, rushing into battle or adventure without considering the consequences. Belligerent and highly competitive, Fire Dragons are constantly on red alert, and their volcanic temper can erupt at any moment.

On the positive side, Fire Dragons believe in getting to the truth of the matter at all costs and they have a passionate, fearless and untiring desire to do good. Inspirational performers and leaders who, in fact, have much to offer other people, they simply need to try to communicate more effectively in order to forge and maintain strong relationships. In the interests of their heart and circulatory system, the organ system of the Fire Element, they are well advised to keep the worst excesses of their explosive tendencies under control.

EARTH DRAGON: 1928, 1988
"Dragon of Pure Virtue"

The Earth Dragon, also known as "yielding Dragon", is quieter and more stable than the average Dragon. Earth Dragons are more patient, less inflammatory and less egocentric. Calming, settled Earth energy (in double quantities as Earth is the Fixed Element for the Dragon, too) grounds this Dragon to make him or her more even-tempered, prudent and realistic.

Earth Dragons earn genuine respect from others because their volatile and controlling characteristics are tempered by logic, reason and a willingness to consult and listen to others. They're sociable individuals with good management skills – and they may even become protective toward those who work for them. Although they're happiest in the position of ruler, they're not dictatorial in their management style. Like Water Dragons, Earth Dragons are interested in working for the common good, and if anything Earth Dragons might well watch out for being just that little bit too restrained, too adaptable or too accommodating of others' wishes, remembering to act on their own instincts, too.

Steady and tenacious, Earth Dragons work hard to succeed. Although their methods might be more logical and considered than other Dragon types, they still have plenty of Dragonly courage, overcoming obstacles to continually improve themselves and ensuring that they, too, become high achievers in this world.

THE TWELVE ANIMAL SIGNS

WORK, CAREER AND MONEY

Visionary; Innovative; Enterprising; Generous; Honest

THE DRAGON IN WORK AND CAREER

Dragons tend to want to be the focus of attention. They seek out power and respect, and are totally prepared to take full responsibility for their actions. Every Dragon wants to be the MD or CEO – and some will achieve exactly that.

Dragons work hard, but they're bossy and hate taking orders from others. In fact, they would rather move on than have to dance to another's tune. People of action, Dragons want to get things done and find it hard to tolerate menial or insignificant work, and may hate having to comply with rules and regulations. Political correctness in the workplace is simply an anathema to these fire-breathing creatures. However, Dragons can be brilliant at thinking up new and better ways of doing things – whether they're called upon to do so, or not. Creating a stir doesn't bother the Dragon, who is glad for the attention.

Dragons are natural leaders, but often with a dictatorial style, which means they may not make great team players. Generally, they lack diplomacy and are fiercely intolerant of group members who don't pull their weight. This person is not a negotiator – for the Dragon, winning a deal is all about outright victory. Dragons will simply fight until they get it all their own way.

In their work and career, Dragons are very future-oriented. They make great entrepreneurs and inventors. They're versatile, disciplined and make sure they're

---

COMMON CAREER POSSIBILITIES

• IT • PR • ADVERTISING • STOCK MARKET • LAW • POLITICS
• CEO • DOCTOR • ENTREPRENEUR • ACTOR • ARCHITECT • ENGINEER
• INVENTOR • PSYCHIATRIST • ARMY OFFICER • SENIOR MANAGER

good at what they do, which makes self-employment a viable option for them. However, the fact that they approach everything without any consideration for the consequences means that when they make a mistake it's often a very big one – at which point, they delegate fixing that mistake to someone else.

THE DRAGON AND MONEY

In Chinese tradition, the dragon enjoys the perfect balance between Heaven and Earth, giving this animal sign a reputation for being able to manifest good fortune and material well-being. Certainly, the Dragon's dedication to work and his or her confidence, dynamism, irrepressibility, and willingness to take risks point to a person who should enjoy financial success.

However, all Dragons tend to have an easygoing attitude toward money – Dragons know that fortunes can disappear as quickly and suddenly as they can appear. It's not pecuniary wealth that ultimately interests the Dragon, but rather the power and status that might go with it.

Dragons do, however, love to spend – both on themselves and on others. Renowned for their generosity, Dragons simply aren't that interested in saving. Unless they have made a career out of it, Dragons don't do financial planning. The combination of being risk-takers and completely lacking in fear means that Dragons can be big gamblers, taking rash and often large-scale chances on a whim. From the stock market to a one-armed bandit, and from Monte Carlo to Las Vegas, the Dragon's fiery love of risk is at its most dangerous with a wad of notes in his or her hand.

However, Dragon types are notoriously honest, principled and trustworthy in financial matters – while they might gamble with their own money, they wouldn't dream of cheating someone else out of theirs. And they would certainly never consider embezzlement or other forms of subterfuge to gain money.

When it comes to their own pockets, Dragons need to rein in their willingness to indulge in high-stakes financial speculation. In rare moments of clarity, they need to remind themselves that their skills of judgment are not as highly developed as their spirit of adventure and their attraction to risk.

PREFERENCES AND WELL-BEING
Never a dull moment

PEOPLE, TASTES AND PASTIMES

Dragons are probably the most free-wheeling of all the animal signs. Self-confident and self-sufficient, they're their own people, rarely influenced by those around them. Indeed, they'll actively avoid conforming. They're impetuous and impatient, and as they seem to suffer from excessively high self-esteem, they rarely allow other people into their lives. Self-righteous and opinionated, Dragons are more likely to find themselves criticized by others than befriended. As a result, they can be somewhat isolated from close human contact.

Despite all this – when they choose to be – Dragons are also charismatic individuals with an irrepressible positivity. Extrovert, flamboyant and exhibitionist, they love talking and are wonderful at entertaining, lapping up the adulation of their guests. However, this soon changes if they're not the centre of attention when they might turn snobbish and critical toward others. If a Dragon does become your friend, you have a totally dependable ally – someone who'll fight your corner with unstoppable energy.

Dragon style is wholly unconventional. Fashion is for mere mortals and the Dragon may be found looking instead for clothes that make a statement, relishing yet another opportunity to show off. Dragons tend to wear items that are not only original, but perhaps even controversial – anything that draws attention.

The home has the potential to cage this fiery creature, but nevertheless the Dragon creates a place to live that is impressive and stylish, and that is decorated to express his or her vibrant personality. Adventure, challenge and danger are what Dragons look for in their pastimes. You'll find them taking vacations in out-of-the-way places – perhaps in extremes of climate or environment – and experimenting with bizarre activities: a Dragon will be the one to make it into the newspapers for achieving some strange feat, such as ironing on a mountain top!

HEALTH AND WELL-BEING
Fixed Element: Earth

Dragon types have a reputation for enjoying good health, vitality and longevity, despite their unrestrained approach to life. This could well be down to the fact that Dragons just don't spend as much time dwelling on problems, worrying, and making mountains out of molehills as most of the other animal signs do. As a result, they have very few anxiety-related ailments.

Equally surprising given the Dragon's general good health is the fact that they're rarely bothered about eating healthily. Dragons are far too busy thinking about how to orchestrate world domination to worry about what they eat. As a result, eating becomes an indiscriminate affair, involving grabbing whatever is to hand – which is often not altogether healthy or high-quality. Luckily, the Dragon tends to be an active person, making him or her less prone to weight gain than others who eat in this way.

In other signs, the Dragon's need to endlessly expend energy and seek out daring adventure might cause stress and illness, but in the Dragon it is too much routine, a restricted or stagnant environment and the absence of stimulation that can cause anxiety. If life becomes monotonous and the Dragon senses deep resistance to any of his or her attempts at promoting change, he or she experiences high levels of frustration and stress, which often manifest as upper-body hypertension, headaches and migraines.

Although Dragons tend to age well, in order to prevent immobility and illness during old age (which would make Dragons feel trapped in their own bodies), they should take positive steps to preserve their good health while they're still young. Dragons should take care to hold back a little instead of overdoing and overindulging. They can use their naturally disciplined and self-sufficient natures to apply themselves to self-help techniques that encourage calm and balance. Meditation, yoga and tai chi are all deeply centring activities that may help the Dragon rein in the excesses of their emotional fieriness. With even a small amount of time each week focused on their own well-being, Dragons can show good powers of recovery.

THE SNAKE

SNAKE YEARS: 1905, 1917, 1929, 1941, 1953, 1965, 1977, 1989, 2001, 2013, 2025
SNAKE HOURS: 0900–1100
FIXED ELEMENT: FIRE   YIN SIGN

Snake people are supposedly very difficult to deceive. The wily Snake has a reputation for being able to find out secrets, plots, scandals or underhand goings-on – and rather than bringing these into the light of day, the Snake keeps them hidden until he or she has used them to his or her own advantage. Snakes can also be slow to let others into their confidence, preferring to keep their own secrets locked safely away from scrutiny. With their sharp eye for nuance and detail, they're good at making cool, detached assessments of situations and people. They have a highly developed sense of intuition that can at times seem psychic.

Although Snakes may seem inert or inactive, and although they prefer to stay silent than risk saying something revealing, they're in fact in a constant state of high alert. They may suddenly lash out – in which case, watch out as their strike may be venomous. Being permanently on guard means that Snakes can internalize their stress, and they can become neurotic and paranoid if they feel insecure. Prone to jealousy and possessiveness, Snakes will silently bear a grudge against those they feel have betrayed them. They have a hedonistic nature, surrounding themselves with power, pleasure and luxury.

The Snake's complementary and opposite sign is the Dragon.

KEYWORDS
• INTENSE • MYSTERIOUS • INSIGHTFUL • SPIRITUAL • SOPHISTICATED
• SENSUOUS • DISCREET • WISE • SEDUCTIVE • TENACIOUS • ELEGANT
• CALCULATING • QUIET • WATCHFUL • RESTRAINED

THE FIVE TYPES OF SNAKE

METAL SNAKE: 1941, 2001
"*Hibernating Snake*"
The Metal Snake is an immensely strong character, with a rigid will and unwavering courage and self-belief – sometimes to the point of over-confidence. Metal Snakes follow their own instincts to get things done, always with the utmost integrity – a rare thing in a Snake.

Metal represents contraction and inwardness, so Metal Snakes are perhaps the most secretive of all. They're always wary and suspicious, and always on the lookout for danger, or for the opportunity to improve themselves or fulfil their wishes and desires. When danger or opportunity presents itself, Metal Snakes can respond with lightning speed.

Never wanting to be tied down by others, Metal Snakes like to be in a position of influence – on the top of the pile – although they'll also help others to rise with them. They achieve supremacy by any means necessary, often using devious tactics or becoming severe or harsh toward others. However, underneath lies an insecure person, with a deeply passionate, romantic and empathetic nature, who can be irrationally envious of other people. This insecurity coupled with the Snake's general tendency to be unable to express him- or herself freely, means that Metal Snakes may turn out to be rather solitary figures. Metal energy does not mix well with solitude, and a kind of gloom may descend over the Metal Snake, who needs to make an effort to revitalize the energy in the lungs and respiration system (the organ system of the Metal Element), through, for example, laughter and physical activity.

Metal Snakes adore luxury and may go overboard to surround themselves with the best of everything and to live the good life, which altogether suits their laid-back natures.

WATER SNAKE: 1953, 2013
"Snake in the Grass"

The Water Snake is a particularly curious, intuitive and insightful person. Like flowing water, Water Snakes can find their way lithely around obstacles. They're also particularly tenacious and persistent and will keep going until they reach the place they want to be. Organized and focused, they're not thrown off course by extraneous matters and are good at business, and with money.

Water Snakes are good judges of character and are more able to get on with other people and to exert influence over them than some of the more introspective Snake types. Their philosophical and understanding natures make Water Snakes charismatic people to be around, and they're especially loving toward their family and close friends. Like all Snakes, they can still be secretive, and they're particularly stubborn when it comes to holding grudges.

Intellectual and culturally sophisticated, Water Snakes place a high level of importance on aesthetics. They like a pleasant environment to live in, and they like to look good. Sensual pleasure is high on the list of priorities for the Water Snake, who can be flirtatious, seductive and hedonistic. Water Snakes are happy to spend their money on anything that makes them look and feel great.

Like still water, Water Snakes can be slow to make decisions. They should take care not to be too passive in life. It's important for Water Snakes to stimulate the energy of the kidneys, the organ system of the Water Element, with lots of healthy, physical activities – and avoid letting energy stagnate through excess.

WOOD SNAKE: 1905, 1965, 2025
"Snake Leaving its Hole"

The harmony-focused Wood Element brings warmth and likeability, kindness and foresight to this less self-centred Snake type. Creative and inventive, and good at organizing information, the Wood Snake is able to consider the "big picture" and use his or her conclusions and foresight to achieve success.

This Snake is the one most concerned for the well-being of others. Idealistic and humanistic, Wood Snakes are motivated by altruism. They notice those who are less well off than they are or who are in need of help. This, combined with their inquisitiveness and genuine interest in others, earns popularity and respect from a greater circle of friends than is available to the other Snake types.

Although they're less egotistical than other Snakes, Wood Snakes tend to be better at talking about themselves and the causes that interest them. They're good at public speaking and are able to gather the support of others. Wood Snakes are naturally more inclined to want to rely on their own means and they'd do well to remember that there's much to be gained in terms of success and emotional stability from listening to the counsel of other people.

Wood Snakes have good taste and discerning habits, enjoying fine arts, music and literature. Personal appearance and tasteful surroundings are very important to them – they believe that others will think better of them and like them more if they're surrounded by lovely things. The Wood Snake's top priority, though, is a stable and harmonious family life, filled with loyal affection. Building a secure environment will greatly help balance the *chi* flowing through the liver, the organ system of the Wood Element.

FIRE SNAKE: 1917, 1977
"Snake in the Pond"

Fire is the fixed Element of the Snake, so this type has a double helping of fiery energy. As a result, the Fire Snake is a particularly intense and dynamic individual who is less prone to the inertia of other Snake types. Fire Snakes are extrovert and voluble, with great charisma. They have high levels of confidence and unshakeable self-belief, which can make them slightly unconventional.

Fire Snakes are natural leaders. Their persuasive natures and irrepressible enthusiasm have great appeal for other people. Lively and animated speakers, Fire Snakes engage others with their words and are able to influence others.

Intensely and strategically ambitious – both in terms of financial and material success and in terms of reputation – they hate to relinquish power and are unwilling to compromise. They focus mainly on themselves and may treat others with criticism, envy, irreverence or suspicion. Their general attitude of self-importance and condescension toward others means that Fire Snakes tend to have a more limited circle of close friends than other Snake types.

Fire Snakes can also suffer from over-intense passions and from aggressiveness, and they may strike out at people from time to time. Further alienating them from the company of others, this temper can lead to ill-health, perhaps affecting the heart and circulation, the organ system of the Fire Element.

EARTH SNAKE: 1929, 1989
"Prosperous Snake"

The Earth Snake is deeply rooted in common sense, creating an individual who can be more straightforward, less deceptive, less fearful and more easy going than general Snake characteristics suggest. Grounded, balanced, calm and confident, the Earth Snake is not as prone to venomous lightning strikes as other Snakes.

Earth Snakes are somewhat analytical beings – solid, systematic and persistent in the way they apply themselves to the tasks in hand. They're patient and practical, bringing about change slowly but reliably, overcoming problems and surmounting obstacles over the course of time. Their shrewdness and logic give them a reputation for being good with money. They build up strong convictions and principles as a result of reliably assessing what goes on and prioritizing what's important – both in their immediate environment and in the world in general.

Sensible and well grounded, Earth Snakes are empathetic, good at communication, and good team players. People trust them (with their money, too), so they tend to be less isolated than some of the other members of the Snake clan.

Like other Snakes, Earth Snakes enjoy the good things in life, but not to so much excess. They do not squander money or resources, even to the point of being a little too risk-averse. Earth Snakes need to develop inner confidence so that slow progress does not become altogether stationary. A static nature can also cause problems with weight gain and blood sugar, or other repercussions for the stomach, spleen and pancreas – the organ system of the Earth Element.

WORK, CAREER AND MONEY

Discreet; Focused; Independent; Logical; Precise

THE SNAKE IN WORK AND CAREER

The Snake person is highly versatile. A quick learner, he or she can easily switch between roles within a chosen career – or indeed have several different successful careers over the course of a working lifetime. Snake types hanker after power, and are good at spotting opportunities for self-advancement. They're very good at using strategy to further themselves, and can be ruthless. On the other hand, they're also skilled at advancing by means of their immense charm and beguiling ways. They don't like to be told they're wrong – and can turn venomous if they're proved to be so. Independent and resourceful, snakes can be successful in self-employment, as well as in the employ of others.

Snakes are scrupulous, paying great attention to detail when gathering information, and they're excellent at problem-solving. Able to look at things in unconventional ways, the Snake can quickly grasp the essential points of a complex issue – this can make them great lawyers or detectives, for example. They enjoy a challenge and will keep a cool head in times of trouble – but don't ever expect a Snake person to get his or her hands dirty.

Snakes have a strong humanitarian streak and do well in service positions. However, with their great need for independence and self-sufficiency, and their unswerving confidence in themselves, Snakes don't make great team players.

COMMON CAREER POSSIBILITIES

• SCIENCE • POLITICS • MUSIC • FASHION • STAGE MAGIC
• FINANCE • DETECTIVE • PSYCHIATRIST • DOCTOR • NUTRITIONIST
• LAWYER • ENTREPRENEUR • ARCHAEOLOGIST • ENGINEER

THE SNAKE AND MONEY

In Chinese astrology, Snakes are considered to be financially fortunate – they're able to accumulate money without too much difficulty. There are probably very good, practical reasons for this traditional view, as Snakes display unshakeable self-belief, and dedicated application to the process of making money. In the pursuit of wealth, Snakes will not want to push themselves too hard: instead, they quietly accumulate pecuniary success by remaining their own person and not being swayed by anyone else's opinion. They're cautious and methodical about the acquisition of money and prepared to do whatever it takes to fill their bank accounts. This means they'll often use guile, and they're certainly not averse to stooping to unscrupulous measures. Irrevocably attached to a luxurious lifestyle, Snakes are motivated by their innate need to surround themselves with the best life has to offer. Like so many animal types that are naturally good with money, Snakes are not interested in money as an end in itself, but more as a means to something that is genuinely important for them.

Snakes have a curiously ambiguous reputation with regard to spreading their wealth around. On the one hand, they're often accused of being spendthrifts – buying frivolous, expensive items both for themselves and for those who are closest to them. If you see a Snake in diamonds, the gems are probably real. On the other hand, Snakes have a reputation for being penny-pinching, especially if they've spent part of their lives without the material possessions they feel they deserve. Both reputations ring true in their own ways. Many Snakes have a little of both approaches: they're happy to spend money on luxury items – the best seats at the theatre, the most expensive clothes and so on – and less happy to spend it on more mundane, utilitarian stuff. If the roof needs fixing or they need to buy a new washing machine, Snakes keep their money tightly stowed away in their pockets until it is absolutely necessary to spend it.

Snakes are well advised to keep their lightning responses under control when it comes to making money, sticking with the slow and careful accumulation of wealth. Impulsive decisions are dangerous for Snakes and their money. Snakes should avoid gambling, or speculating with any degree of high financial risk.

THE TWELVE ANIMAL SIGNS

PREFERENCES AND WELL-BEING
Guarding secrets

PEOPLE, TASTES AND PASTIMES

Snake people are well known for their conflicting needs to be sociable and to be alone. When they feel like company, they enjoy small, carefully selected groups of people whom they trust. When they feel like some quiet, private time, they do not want to be disturbed by anyone else at all. Snakes aren't interested in small talk or chit-chat; they like to get right to the heart of the matter, winkling out others' best-kept secrets and relishing the latest piece of gossip. There is no *quid pro quo* in these exchanges, however – Snakes are fiercely efficient at keeping secure their own intimate details. They also greatly dislike being given advice.

Snakes guard their friendships jealously. If anyone dares ignite their possessive nature, or equally if anyone disappoints them or lets them down, Snakes may strike with a flare of their angry temper. And even if the temper itself passes quickly, the legendary Snake sulk may set in for a while.

Vain and image-conscious, Snakes do, as a result, have excellent taste. Their clothes are elegant and glamorous, and both men and women like to appear ravishing. Snakes know just how to put together the perfect combination of clothing and accessories, always getting the balance right, without appearing garish or over the top. They create a home that is comfortable, decorated with high-quality furnishings that reflect their sophisticated tastes.

On vacation, Snakes search for both comfort and culture. They seek out locations that are away from busy places and preferably close to nature so that they can indulge their need for privacy and for peace and quiet. At home they spend their time relaxing and resting, perhaps punctuated with theatre visits or meals out in good restaurants. You may even find them pampering themselves with a treatment at an exclusive spa – after all, looking good is always important for the beautiful, wily Snake.

HEALTH AND WELL-BEING
Fixed Element: Fire

In almost all areas of their lives, Snakes have apparently conflicting tendencies, and that is as true for their health and well-being as it is for their need to be sociable or alone. The health of the Snake, like everything else about him or her, can be as mysterious and as dualistic as ever.

Snakes do not have a general tendency to worry. Rather, they have a healthy ability to switch off and tune out. They aren't overly concerned with what others think of them and have a well-balanced view of themselves and confidence in their ability. All this points to strong emotional well-being. However, their possessive and jealous natures, along with their needs for freedom and for peace and quiet (particularly in the home), and order and discipline in all areas of their lives, mean that they can quickly become highly stressed when these character traits come under pressure. The result is often a nervous response that is a huge over-reaction – an angry temper or one of several nervous complaints, such as palpitations or high blood pressure, which are linked with the heart and circulation, the organ system of Fire.

In order to preserve a balanced flow of *chi* through their circulation, Snakes should take care to avoid gluttony. Their attraction to sensual pleasure, including rich, fatty foods and the finest wine, and their love of sedentary pursuits and of inactivity, can lead them to overindulge somewhat. This can result in weight gain later in life and put strain on the heart and circulation.

Although Snakes might not indulge in many active pursuits, they do commit themselves fully to work and it's important that they take regular rests from it in order to recharge their batteries. They should bear in mind that physical activity provides release for the body and that it doesn't need to be high-impact aerobics – gentle walks through the countryside or regular swimming sessions can be both relaxing and active. Equally, pursuits that combine relaxation, de-stressing and detoxification make ideal components of the Snake's health regime. Yoga, meditation or tai chi, or alternative health treatments such as shiatsu, Thai massage or reflexology, all fall into this category.

THE HORSE

HORSE YEARS: 1906, 1918, 1930, 1942, 1954, 1966, 1978, 1990, 2002, 2014, 2026
HORSE HOURS: 1100–1300
FIXED ELEMENT: FIRE **YANG SIGN**

Those born under the auspices of the Horse sign always want to be on the move. They constantly seek to gallop forward in life, looking for new pastures. In wide-open spaces they gather their pack – and preferably lead it.

Easily bored, and excited by challenge, Horses are highly motivated to seek success. They enjoy the reckless adventure of taking a risk – sometimes a little too much – but may be inclined not to see the risk through. Most Horses happily pick up new ventures and then lose interest and drop them when something else takes their interest. Taking the long-term view is not their speciality, and if something doesn't turn out well, they can become despondent and disillusioned.

Nevertheless, Horses have sharp minds and can be excellent multi-taskers, so they have much to offer the projects to which they do commit. Straightforward and full of ideas, they may become stubborn on some issues and will rear up angrily if someone threatens or challenges their opinions.

Horses are celebrated for their passionate natures, but they may lack self-control – a Horse will never guarantee stability in a relationship. They will not, though, ever mix work and pleasure.

The Horse's complementary and opposite sign is the Sheep.

KEYWORDS

• LIVELY • INDEPENDENT • EXUBERANT • WITTY • ALERT
• HONEST • VIVACIOUS • FUN • CHEERFUL • DRIVEN • ENTHUSIASTIC
• GUILELESS • SELF-CENTRED • CHANGEABLE • IMPULSIVE

THE FIVE TYPES OF HORSE

METAL HORSE: 1930, 1990
"Horse at the Palace Gates"

The Metal Element brings wildness, boldness and strength to the idealistic Horse. More strong-willed and determined than the other Horse types, Metal Horses are particularly wary of commitment. They're reluctant to settle down with a particular person or in a particular place, and hate the idea of becoming restricted or tamed in any way.

Perhaps the overriding characteristic of Metal Horses is their addiction to variety and change. At almost any sign of commitment, Metal Horses will change company, lovers, employment and environment. They have a strong focus on their own wants and needs, which are inherently affected by their restless and impetuous natures. They love adventure and the thrill of something new, and they dislike dull or repetitive situations – and they're undaunted by challenges. Metal Horses are confident, but perhaps not quite as confident as it may at first appear.

As long as they do not feel tied down, Metal Horses are able to sustain their relationships or partnerships, keeping them interesting by using their characteristic romance and passion. In fact, as long as they can keep their inherent tactlessness at bay, Metal Horses are able to build good relationships. At work, if they can engage with people and then be allowed to get on with their tasks and be appreciated for completing them, they're perfectly happy in teams with others.

Metal Horses are intelligent and especially impetuous creatures. They bring to the table an unrivalled enthusiasm and a brilliance for turning their ideas into action. However, their scattered attentions can mean they miss out on making the most of their ideas by constantly being on the go. They need to work hard at persistence and take care not to wear themselves out – which can badly affect the lungs and respiration, the organ system of the Metal Element.

WATER HORSE: 1942, 2002
"Army Horse"

Flexible and adaptable, the Water Horse can always derive the maximum advantage from any situation.

Probably the least decisive of the Horse clan, Water Horses are characterized by their spontaneity. Frequently changing their mood, mind and direction, they follow the fluidity of their heart, often allowing situations to get out of control. Their lack of firm direction, together with the fact they don't appear to be in tune with those around them, can be antagonizing and unsettling for other people, making personal relationships something of a challenge.

However, Water Horses value human contact and can be idealistic about relationships, despite their preoccupation with themselves. They're gifted at communication – witty and entertaining, cheerful and chatty – so they easily win people over. Water qualities also give this Horse excellent business acumen – Water Horses have a reputation for being particularly perceptive in work situations, quickly spotting opportunities for improvement or advancement.

Like the other Horses, Water Horses occasionally lose their good cheer, becoming negative and despondent. This can be an emotional function of weakened *chi* in the kidneys, the organ system of the Water Element. Water Horses benefit from reining in their impatience and their impetuous tendencies, endeavouring to see things from other people's points of view, and thinking things through in advance in order to prepare better for future eventualities.

WOOD HORSE: 1954, 2014
"Horse in the Clouds"

The stabilizing effect of the Wood Element on the otherwise highly excitable Horse produces a calmer, gentler and more patient Horse type. Wood also creates a Horse that can think innovatively, imaginatively and creatively, while at the same time retaining the Horse's generally disciplined mental acuity.

More consistent and less changeable than other types, Wood Horses are better able than other types to see objectives through to their conclusions.

And because Wood Horses also have superior people skills, they're effective team members, generating understanding and co-operation among their colleagues. This, in turn, makes Wood Horses all the more influential.

Wood Horses tend to be more committed than others in their clan when it comes to personal relationships. Sociable and optimistic and possessed of a zest for life, Wood Horses don't want to be tamed, but equally they don't have such a need to be dominant. As a result their partnerships tend to be much more stable.

You'll never see a Wood Horse shy away from unconventional situations – he or she is happy to gallop forward into the unknown. Wood Horses enjoy creative innovation and new ventures, which, coupled with their capacity for following through with their work, means they can be very successful. As long as they can keep things relatively under control, that is. Wood Horses can become stressed or anxious if they feel things are slipping out of kilter – which is a key emotional aspect of the liver, the organ system of the Wood Element.

FIRE HORSE: 1906, 1966, 2026
"Travelling Horse"
With Fire already present as its fixed Element, this type of Horse has double Fire influence. In ancient Chinese lore, Fire Horses represented conflict and tyranny and a Fire Horse daughter was particularly unwelcome, as no one would want to marry her. The Chinese believed that Fire Horses would experience only extremes of fortune – total success or total failure, fame or disgrace, wealth or poverty, and so on. Today, of course, we interpret these beliefs in more moderate terms.

Double Fire influence does imply extreme volatility. Hyperactive and adventurous, Fire Horses may completely defy convention and demand total freedom. Life has to be fast, and possibly dangerous: Fire Horses have lightning-quick responses to everything. They're classic over-achievers, dramatic and forceful in reaching their goals. More than any other Horse type, Fire Horses' attention is constantly shifting; they're addicted to change, picking up new projects, new passions and new directions. They'll keep multiple strands going at once, but they'll rarely see any of them through.

Nevertheless, Fire Horses are at heart principled individuals. They have a magnetism that draws people to them and they love to lead (and hate to follow). However, if you're following a Fire Horse, you'll need to work hard to keep up – he or she will be off at a gallop at a moment's notice, and who knows in which direction? As a result, Fire Horses have complex and tempestuous relationships.

With their flair and intellect, Fire Horses may come close to genius, but if they don't rein themselves in, they risk burn-out, upsetting the balance of *chi* in their heart and circulation, the organ system of the Fire Element.

EARTH HORSE: 1918, 1978
"Horse in the Stable"

The gathering and settling influence of the Earth Element reduces the frenetically nomadic tendencies of the Horse to produce a more steady and stable, and less highly strung individual. The Earth Horse is practical and sensible, less dynamic but more contented – more of a workhorse and less of a thoroughbred.

Earth Horses think before they act, weighing up their options and playing things safer than other Horse types. They may become rather indecisive, particularly on more trivial matters. However, they're shrewd when it comes to money and material wealth. Prudent, and good at gathering information, Earth Horses have sound business sense, and their reputation for dependability draws attention of the right sort. They're very interested in self-advancement.

Considerate and compassionate, Earth Horses tend to be rather more conciliatory in nature than other Horse types. They're happy to take advice, and will even take orders; and they're principled, responsible, sociable and sympathetic. Earth Horses are good company, with earthy good humour.

Characteristically indecisive in love, once they do make a decision, Earth Horses do so with full commitment. They enjoy a harmonious home life, and they tend to accumulate success and material well-being slowly but steadily. Consequently, they're less prone to nervous complaints than other Horses, but they may wish to guard against weight gain in later life – a hazard for those born under the Earth Element with its influence over the stomach, spleen and pancreas.

WORK, CAREER AND MONEY

Experimental; Pioneering; Versatile; Hardworking; Opportunistic

THE HORSE IN WORK AND CAREER

Horses love learning, which means they're quick to adapt to new roles and relish the challenges of hard, particularly physical, work. Innovative and experimental, Horses are pioneers, initiating new projects and keeping their colleagues enthused through their own optimistic and positive attitude toward their endeavours.

At home in a group, Horses like working with other people, and they're good talkers and communicators – but they're likely to rear in anger if they feel they're being told what to do. When in charge, they can be inspiring leaders – although employees should steel themselves against the Horse's lack of tact. They also lack attention to detail and may not stay focused on boring or repetitive work, so their ideal job gives them a degree of authority, freedom and independence, allowing them to be improvisational before handing over to someone else to take care of the fine print. They aren't great at timekeeping. Horses work well in partnership, where they can provide the ideas and multi-task, while a more organized partner makes sure they adhere to the detail.

Horses are well advised to work on their staying power, on being more prepared to see tasks through rather than starting out on something at full gallop and then dropping it when they encounter a problem or when another activity catches their eye. They should look for jobs that specialize in initiation or require

---

COMMON CAREER POSSIBILITIES

• COMMUNICATIONS • CONSTRUCTION • SPORTS • ADVERTISING • SALES
• PR • TRANSLATOR • LIBRARIAN • INTERVIEWER • RESEARCHER
• TRAVEL GUIDE • PERFORMER • ARTIST • JOURNALIST • COUNSELLOR

them constantly to come up with new ideas, but long-term project managers, they're not. Nonetheless, Horses are fully committed in the pursuit of their own careers, even though they won't have anything resembling an overall game plan.

THE HORSE AND MONEY

Horses are enthusiastic about everything they like to do in life, and making money is something they like to do. As they're extremely industrious, Horses generally make good financial progress, accumulating wealth and material possessions over the course of their lives. They believe in being well paid for the efforts they've put in and they have a strong capacity for being opportunistic. Their unconventional natures can lead to untapped sources of finance, and they can be tough bargainers.

However, Horses are also fickle, prone to changing direction or moving on at a whim. This means they're not always well-organized, particularly when it comes to financial matters. Easily bored or distracted, Horses can be hopeless at keeping tabs on their financial position – ask a Horse how much money is in his or her bank account, and you'll receive only a quizzical frown in response. In business and home life, keeping accounts is anathema. To make financial matters worse, Horses are the most headstrong animals in the Chinese Zodiac and are not open to advice or counsel of any kind – including financial advice.

Subtlety is not the Horse's strong suit and no Horse will win a financial negotiation by guile. However, Horses can be persuasive in a more straightforward and uncompromising way – they'll simply stick to their guns, and they're not unknown to be unscrupulous in their tactics. Horses may well be attracted to the idea of financial risk or speculation, just for the excitement and thrill of it, but they're well advised not to do any large-scale, risky investment – their lack of focus on the detail means they won't have done the necessary homework to be able to discriminate between a good gamble and a bad one.

Horses enjoy spending money, but they don't tend to plan far enough ahead to be entirely focused on what their money can really buy them. They spend as they go and, when the money is used up, they go out and earn some more.

PREFERENCES AND WELL-BEING
Finding the spirit of adventure

PEOPLE, TASTES AND PASTIMES

Vivacious and hyperactive, Horse types love chatting to friends, socializing and partying. However, never let the conversation become mundane or you might discover they've vanished from one party only for them to reappear soon after at another – probably more interesting – one. Relentlessly entertaining and witty, Horses are born performers who love being the centre of attention. They tend to have a lot of friends, and once they've made a connection with you, you'll probably know a horse for life – if you can keep up with them, that is. They're constantly on the lookout for new activities and interests, so are keen to join groups and societies that offer the opportunity for new and exciting adventures.

However, the Horse's sociability is not about his or her profound interest in others – it's all about the Horse being able to fulfil a need to have lots of things going on at once. Horses often start off social trends. They also have a great sense of gamesmanship, with a good-natured competitive streak that makes them fun to spar with. And if they display a sudden, temperamental outburst – often over something others think is inconsequential – it's quickly over.

As friends, then, Horses are changeable, erratic, unpredictable, unpunctual, unconventional and apparently whimsical (although not in their own minds) – and they can have very strong opinions and fixed views about everything. If you can get past all that, you do, however, have a true and steadfast friend.

At home, Horses love to entertain, but they hate to clear up afterward – Horses are not keen on household chores. They favour active pastimes that provide plenty of adventure, excitement and perhaps even danger – although they would probably be oblivious to that. They particularly enjoy physical activity, such as running or dancing, and anything that involves high speeds. They also love to travel, preferably off the beaten track and probably on a last-minute whim, happily roughing it if there's no hotel bed to sleep in. However, being the loyal friends they are, they'll always carry their cellphone to keep up with their nearest and dearest and the lifelong friends they have scattered far and wide.

HEALTH AND WELL-BEING
Fixed Element: Fire

Strong and healthy, Horses conduct their lives in ways that firmly establish their physical and mental well-being. They enjoy plenty of healthy physical exercise in the fresh air; they keep themselves busy and are unlikely to have periods of neurosis or introspection that would result in them locking themselves away. More than anything, Horses take a cheerful attitude to life, habitually finding a positive response to most of what happens to them. They approach their constant search for pastures new in an uncomplicated and happy-go-lucky way, which provides them with a steady accumulation of happiness.

Paradoxically, Horses' positive, non-morbid, non-methodical approach to life can at times cause, or at least exacerbate, health issues. The Horse is unlikely to even register encroaching illness, which can mean that he or she ignores (or doesn't even notice) warning signs that would enable him or her to take steps to halt poor health in its tracks. As a result, Horses might suddenly find themselves going to the doctor with a complaint that puts them out of action for a while.

Despite their generally carefree make-up, Horses also have a tendency toward nervousness. Being unable to get out and about, being physically inactive, feeling channelled or constrained, or feeling isolated will all bring on stress and anxiety. This can adversely affect the flow of *chi* through the heart and circulation, the organ system of the Horse's fixed Element, Fire. Horses are prone to relieving stress by drowning their sorrows with a glass of wine or two, or even using medication to help them relax. Instead, they would be well advised to get out into the fresh air and shake off the blues with a hearty walk through the countryside or a burst of activity, such as a run. But they should be careful not to overdo it. A good balance between activity and rest, and some healthy meals, rather than endless grazing, are the keys to a Horse's health.

THE SHEEP

SHEEP YEARS: 1907, 1919, 1931, 1943, 1955, 1967, 1979, 1991, 2003, 2015, 2027
SHEEP HOURS: 1300–1500
FIXED ELEMENT: EARTH   YIN SIGN

The Sheep is a classic example of a yin sign – yielding, mild-mannered, interested in beauty and aesthetics, lacking in aggression and not terribly practical. Sheep need security and are made nervous by the unexpected. They tend to hate conflict and confrontation and they'll retreat to a safe place – such as their home or their work – if they think there's anything daunting or threatening on the horizon.

This capacity for worry extends to the way they feel treated, too. Sheep can be oversensitive and will hold back from expressing their own emotions. As a result they can build up internal resentment, giving them a reputation for being sulky. Equally, they can be naïve, leaving them open to exploitation. When seriously crossed they may become more like a ram – a dangerous opponent and a powerful ally. All five Sheep types are noted for their strong interest in, love for and capability in cultural and creative pursuits, such as artistry, literature and matters of intellect. They look for sophistication in their homes and pastimes.

Taking a meandering approach to reaching their goals, Sheep like to exercise choice and hate feeling penned in. When prepared to step beyond their comfort zones, they're capable of capitalizing on countless opportunities for greatness.

The Sheep's complementary and opposite sign is the Horse.

KEYWORDS
• STABLE • COMPANIONABLE • IDEALISTIC • ACQUIESCENT
• FAMILY-MINDED • KIND • SENSITIVE • FORGIVING • NURTURING
• GENEROUS • SINCERE • RESERVED • PLACID • YIELDING • FUSSY

THE FIVE TYPES OF SHEEP

METAL SHEEP: 1931, 1991
"Prosperous Sheep"

The toughest of the Sheep types, the Metal Sheep might be considered closer in nature to a ram or a goat than a gentle lamb. Appearing self-confident and self-sufficient, the Metal Sheep is generally more independent and less gregarious than others in the Sheep clan. Metal Sheep may be more passionate and idealistic people, with stronger and more complex emotions. They also have sharper minds, which serves them well in business, and a more rigid or controlling nature.

Less sociable than the rest of the flock, Metal Sheep choose their friends and professional contacts judiciously. With many other people, they may seem somewhat aloof, severe or controlling, and sometimes gloomy – a product of blocked *chi* in the lungs and respiration, the organ system of Metal. Nevertheless, they still have the Sheep's capacity for kindliness and compassion.

Metal Sheep are strongly passionate, a trait that finds expression in the typical Sheep's love of aesthetics, artistry and culture. They're the most resistant to change of all Sheep types and may particularly seek a stable, secure and harmonious life without extremes, being prepared to work hard to achieve this.

Loyal and constant in their close relationships, Metal Sheep make committed partners who are willing to do whatever it takes to make a relationship work. They're utterly devoted to their family.

Like mountain sheep, Metal Sheep have a tough constitution and are extremely hardworking, but they can be worriers – the Metal Element exacerbates their tendency to turn inward and retreat during times of trouble. Prioritizing the stable and harmonious environment that they crave provides a bastion against this. It would also help if they could let go of their inclination toward controlling others, facilitating a more harmonious journey toward their goals.

WATER SHEEP: 1943, 2003
"Sheep in the Flock"

The Water Element enhances the Sheep's naturally easy-going nature, creating a type that is particularly gentle, calm and reflective. An undemonstrative person, with a quiet manner, the Water Sheep in fact has hidden emotional depths and may become rather talkative in safe environments around those he or she trusts. Generally, though, Water Sheep are timid and lacking in self-confidence – a result of an imbalance of *chi* in the kidneys, the organ system of the Water Element.

The great strength of the Water Sheep is his or her ability to communicate. Motivated by the need to do good for others, Water Sheep are terribly diplomatic. Consequently, they're easy to get along with, attracting the affection – and even protection – of others. They make strong friendships, and may come to depend heavily on their friends. In love, finding someone to be adventurous with will help them enjoy experiences they might otherwise choose to avoid.

Water Sheep veer away from drama and are not hugely ambitious, but they create their own happiness by steadily working away to achieve success and stability, and to provide enough money so they can indulge in the pastimes they enjoy. The refined artistic tastes of the Sheep manifest in the Water Sheep as a love of gentle and subtle art forms, such as ballet. Although they have diverse interests, and may be prone to oversensitivity, generally speaking Water Sheep are creatures of habit. They're people who truly live by the Taoist philosophy of going with the flow and taking the path of least resistance.

WOOD SHEEP: 1955, 2015
"Serious Sheep"

The Wood Element brings out the innate Sheep qualities of caring, nurturing and sensitivity. Principled and wise, Wood Sheep are serious thinkers, but their reserved nature means that they do not foist their wisdom on others.

Indeed, Wood Sheep may be so reserved as to seem rather disengaged from the goings on around them. But with their gentle treatment of others, they're nevertheless able to make plenty of friends, who openly appreciate the unfailing support that a Wood Sheep friend will be prepared to offer – and they extend to the Wood Sheep their support and counsel in return. Wood Sheep may be particularly good at establishing and maintaining one-to-one relationships. Affectionate, romantic and with a reputation for passionate sexual relationships, Wood Sheep place a high emphasis on finding a partner for life whom they adore, and who will adore them, too.

At times Wood Sheep would be well advised to be more careful with their time and energy. They may give too much of themselves and be too keen to give in to others in order to avoid a scene. They can be so trusting and keen to please that others may take advantage of them. For the best results in life, they may need to treat those outside their close circle with a little more caution, and they would also do well to approach some situations with a little more humour.

To ease the flow of *chi* through the liver and gall bladder, the organ system of the Wood Element, Wood Sheep should try to spend time among nature.

FIRE SHEEP: 1907, 1967, 2027
"Sheep Alone"

The Fire Sheep is the liveliest and most extrovert of the Sheep family. The Sheep's naturally timid nature and general vulnerability are muted by the energy of Fire, creating Sheep who are more capable of pushing themselves forward, more independent and self-sufficient and less reliant on the herd. None of this may be obvious, of course – the Fire Sheep may still hide behind a shy façade.

Determined and ambitious, Fire Sheep have intense, spontaneous natures and are not afraid to experiment or follow their own impulses. They're far more likely to speak up if something displeases or upsets them, making them less "sheepish" generally and far less prone to sulking than other Sheep types. They'll also ask more questions. Persuasive instigators, with the general likeability of the Sheep, they make successful business people. All this, of course, within the parameters of retreating to their beloved peace and quiet at the end of the day.

The Sheep interest in creativity manifests in the Fire Sheep as a love of more dramatic and outgoing art forms, such as theatre or opera. They like to indulge their taste for luxury, socializing and travel, which may tempt them into spending more money than they can afford. Fire Sheep are deeply passionate, although they may keep their passion contained only for it to burst out unexpectedly. In romantic and sexual relationships, they're more dynamic than other Sheep types.

Fire Sheep may become unrealistic in their expectations, which can make them a little moody. They should allow the quiet nature of the Sheep to come through so that they don't overdo things, and thereby create an imbalance of *chi* in the heart and circulation, the organ system of the Fire Element.

EARTH SHEEP: 1919, 1979
"Sheep in the Pasture"
With Earth as the Sheep's fixed Element, the Earth Sheep experiences double Earth influence, producing a solid, patient, grounded and hardworking type, who lives in the present moment. Earth Sheep especially need to find stability and security and may tend to be cautious and to hide their emotions. More tenacious than others in the Sheep clan, they have a quiet determination to succeed.

At the same time, Earth Sheep are self-sufficient and therefore less dependent on others. As friends, they're loyal, responsible and helpful – and therefore popular. They have a relatively optimistic nature, tending to look for the positive in any situation, and are humorous. Nevertheless, their inherent insecurity means they don't take kindly to criticism.

Earth Sheep place the greatest emphasis of all on their home: a place to retreat to from the outside world is everything they work for. Tasteful artefacts and all the trappings of the good life decorate this sanctuary, where Earth Sheep can go to overcome insecurity and to manage their tendency to worry. By spending time in this safe place, preferably with a loving, supportive partner who understands the delicate nature of the Sheep, Earth Sheep are able to nourish their overall emotional well-being. The Earth Element is associated with the organ system of the stomach, spleen and pancreas. Regular exercise and moderating a tendency to graze are important for an Earth Sheep's health, particularly his or her weight, and especially in later years.

WORK, CAREER AND MONEY

Co-operative; Passive; Creative; Informal; Team player

THE SHEEP IN WORK AND CAREER

At work, the Sheep is in principle flexible, adaptable, versatile and eager to please – although not without several provisos. Sheep workers are happiest and most effective when they're in a community – they're not at all content working on their own. Natural team players, they'll play an active role in and be supportive of the group dynamic. Their gentle presence and empathetic nature can smooth the waters of collective working if other members of the group create ripples.

With their innately meandering way of doing things, Sheep are happy to be given direction, responding well to an assertive manager, who can take the responsibility for decisions away from them. However, direction is not the same as being given orders, and Sheep don't like to be barked at or have demands made of them – and they definitely don't like to be criticized. Sheep work best in a lively environment that provides freedom and a degree of flexibility, and are unhappiest when things become dull or routine or if they have to adhere to strict schedules. Above all, they'll avoid office conflict at all costs.

Artistic or other creative jobs are the most satisfying for all Sheep types, as are jobs that enable them to care for or otherwise help other people. Sheep are not necessarily interested in leadership or high-ranking positions, which they can find highly stressful. Sheep view being happy to follow rather than lead as a

---

COMMON CAREER POSSIBILITIES

• ARCHITECTURE • LANDSCAPE GARDENING • INTERIOR DESIGN • CARE • STYLIST • AUTHOR • FLORIST • NURSE • ARTIST • LIBRARIAN • MUSICIAN • RESEARCHER • ARTS ADMINISTRATOR • ADVERTISING EXECUTIVE

strength, not a weakness – it's a way to express their own true nature. As the home is such a happy and fulfilling place for them, Sheep make highly successful home-makers – a job they approach with relish.

In career-type jobs, even if they don't seek promotion, Sheep will often experience steady advancement in their chosen path, usually through opportunities that simply present themselves. This is partly because their good natures enable them to cultivate good relationships with people who may help them along their way, and partly because Sheep are subtler and cleverer manipulators than most people – including themselves – give them credit for.

THE SHEEP AND MONEY

Not terribly interested in money for its own sake, Sheep are nevertheless pretty good at handling it. Sheep foster good relations with others, building up contacts simply as a result of the naturally generous and kind ways in which they deal with people. As Sheep don't openly show canniness or any sign that they have one eye on the outcome of a situation (and most of the time, they don't), they win the trust of others easily. Happily, their list of contacts just seems to include people who bear gifts or have money – benefactors and patrons, and even the deceased who bestow inheritances.

All this is just as well, for Sheep have a reputation for extravagance, which seems to belie their otherwise meek, quiet and undemonstrative ways. However, it is, in fact, very much in keeping with their well-known penchant for refined and sophisticated experiences and high art. Sheep enjoy spending money on attending the best cultural and artistic events, and purchasing exquisite adornments for their up-market homes. As they must always look their best, they may spend a lot on high-quality clothing and personal grooming. And, of course, they love to mark every special occasion by splashing out – and are very often in the right place to benefit from others splashing out, too!

With their innate willingness to spend money, Sheep can benefit from the presence of a partner or other close person who can help them keep their need for extravagance within realistic limits – at least until the next windfall arrives.

THE TWELVE ANIMAL SIGNS

PREFERENCES AND WELL-BEING
Feeling safe and secure

PEOPLE, TASTES AND PASTIMES

Sheep tend very much to be people people. They love being around other people, are companionable, and seem to need little or no time alone. Considerate, generous and sensitive, they love entertaining, happily hosting any kind of party, whether it's a dinner for a few close friends or a more gregarious affair with music and dancing. Being homebodies, they're certainly happier and feel safest being the ones to entertain rather than visiting others. They love group activities, but prefer to stay out of the limelight – for example, taking a chorus role in choirs or amateur dramatics societies.

Sheep generally divide their friendships into two camps. They have a social circle, whom they'll invite to their bigger, gatherings, but never let into their confidence; and also a closer circle, who are the most trusted and familiar individuals to whom they might – if they have to – bare their soul. They're incurable romantics – always on the lookout for "the one".

Emotionally affected by their surroundings, Sheep thrive only when their home offers a place of absolute security. On their walls hang beautiful photographs of their loved ones (preferably in tasteful frames), and their kitchens may show the trappings of a warm, homely environment: beautiful baking utensils, the best cookery books, and so on – anything that makes this feel like a safe place to come back to. Their love of art may show in their homes, as well as in their own image and appearance – the Sheep is among the best-dressed of the animal signs. As Sheep are both creative and fussy, "creative adjustment" is their speciality – expect them to redecorate frequently.

For recreation and vacation, Sheep enjoy, first and foremost, relaxing at home. They like travelling, but not alone – preferring to go away with their extended family or other loved ones, so that they're surrounded by a secure network of people. For the Sheep, a package vacation or other organized trip, perhaps close to water, takes the stress out of having to make decisions – as long as there isn't too strict a timetable. Familiar places, rich with art and culture, provide the perfect destinations for the Sheep, especially if there's interesting shopping available, too.

HEALTH AND WELL-BEING
Fixed Element: Earth

Their gentle manner and delicate way of handling relationships can make Sheep seem much more physically vulnerable than they really are. They're actually pretty robust. Their generally serene approach to life and their easy-going natures with regard to personal progression ensure that they minimize the pressure they put themselves under and so enhance their general well-being. However, Sheep themselves sometimes fail to appreciate their own inner strength, which can cause them to worry, beginning a cycle of anxiety that, if it escalates, can undermine their health.

Discord, spending too much time alone, or instability at home or in a partnership are the most stressful situations for Sheep to find themselves in. They're also not very good at denying themselves rich foods, and aren't terribly proactive when it comes to physical exercise. The common manifestations of the Sheep's nervous temperament and unhealthy lifestyle involve the digestive system, unstable blood-sugar levels (leading to energy highs and lows, and mood swings) and problems with the stomach, spleen and pancreas – the organ system associated with the Earth Element.

When they're unwell, Sheep love being looked after and made a fuss of, which in itself points to ways in which Sheep can avoid ill-health: reassurance from those around them and having a secure home life with a loving partner keep them well. However, they also need to moderate their food intake, especially sugar-laden food and drink, and take proper exercise, which doesn't mean a gentle meander, but a heart-pounding stride! Swimming, yoga and Pilates, practised regularly, will of course help, too.

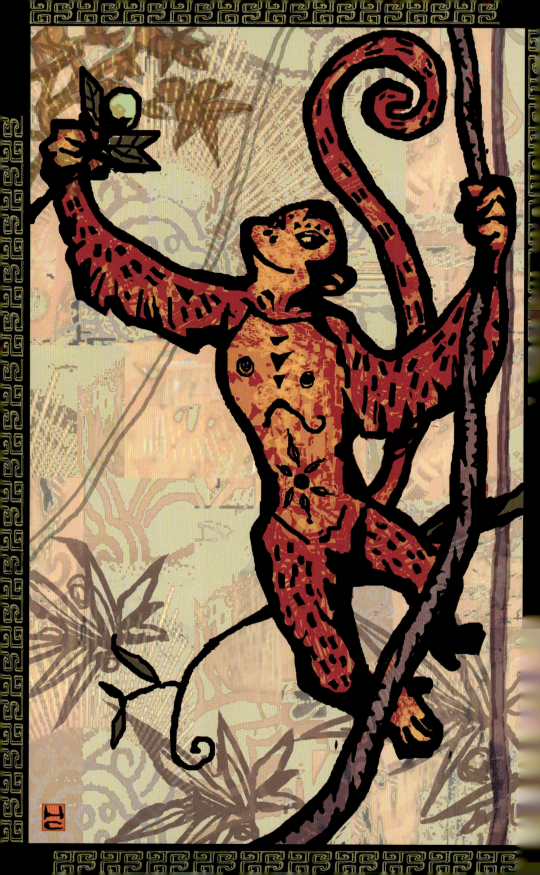

THE MONKEY

MONKEY YEARS: 1908, 1920, 1932, 1944, 1956, 1968, 1980, 1992, 2004, 2016, 2028
MONKEY HOURS: 1500–1700
FIXED ELEMENT: METAL   YANG SIGN

Monkey people are quick and clever. They constantly enjoy new diversions, new experiences and new challenges and they simply can't stand being bored. As a result they're very easily distracted, swinging from one thing to another, and responding to situations in instinctive ways. Monkeys detest routine.

Rather as we might expect, Monkeys are constantly getting up to mischief – and they have an infuriating knack of being able to talk their way out of trouble. They're experts in self-preservation: a Monkey will always know the escape route. Gregarious and nosy, Monkeys don't like being alone and will integrate themselves into groups of strangers with unrivalled confidence.

Despite their great charm, Monkeys are not universally popular. They lack empathy, diplomacy and understanding, and they wouldn't rule out deceit as an acceptable tactic to further their own ends. Others may view them as superficial, but actually they're deeply affected by criticism. This can make them spiteful – they're much more at home with praise, and always believe they deserve it.

Monkeys bring to the world the utmost in talent and ingenuity, with an ability to motivate others to be just as enthusiastic and inspired as they are.

The Monkey's complementary and opposite sign is the Rooster.

KEYWORDS

• INGENIOUS • QUICK-WITTED • NIMBLE • HUMOROUS • INVENTIVE
• ADAPTABLE • CLEVER • IMAGINATIVE • INQUISITIVE • FUN-LOVING
• MISCHIEVOUS • TRICKSTER • RESTLESS • DEVIOUS • SPITEFUL

THE FIVE TYPES OF MONKEY

METAL MONKEY: 1920, 1980
"Monkey in the Fruit Tree"
The double influence of Metal in this Monkey makes him or her especially focused, sharp and determined. Particularly dynamic and lively, Metal Monkeys are firmly dedicated to their cause and have the willpower to make sure they see things through. Metal influence also brings passion, ambition, business ability and independence to the Monkey and makes this Monkey more self-sufficient and tolerant of solitude. Metal also adds wisdom and logic to the Monkey's general quick-wittedness.

Good at making sound investments, Metal Monkeys have a relentless drive to improve their financial and material well-being. They're equally driven toward self-improvement, making them hardworking people who will not compromise on their way to the top. Persuasive and influential, they're able to enrol others to help with their ambitious projects, further improving their own rates of success.

Where romance is concerned, Metal Monkeys are celebrated for their ardent passion and their loyalty. However, they're likely to dominate, which can cause some power struggles. Metal Monkeys should try to compromise by offering at least some of the power in the relationship to their partner.

Metal Monkeys tend to be excessively self-absorbed. Their communication skills aren't up to the usual Monkey standard – they simply don't feel the need to explain themselves, and they have fixed views and are outspoken about them.

Metal Monkeys' restless pursuit of their own agendas means that they're rarely satisfied, making them actually somewhat nervous people. In the interests of their health, and in particular the health of their lungs and respiration (the organ system of the Metal Element), they are well advised to try to lighten up, become more open-minded and less forceful, and be careful not to overdo things.

THE MONKEY 猴

WATER MONKEY: 1932, 1992
"Elegant Monkey"

The flowing qualities of the Water Element create a Monkey who is more sensitive, diplomatic and changeable than the other Monkey types, and also more inscrutable – beneath the surface lie hidden depths we may never understand.

Water Monkeys like to connect and engage with other people, in the hope that both they and others will benefit. Observant and interested, and good at questioning and listening, clever Water Monkeys can draw people into their confidence with an air of straightforward openness, making them seem less tricky that the other Monkey variants. However, they may also be inclined to push their interest too far, and have a reputation for meddling.

Beneath the surface Water Monkeys harbour sensitivities that mean they may be easily offended or wounded by the words or actions of other people. Water Monkeys are very good at keeping these still waters hidden, only occasionally reaching the point of having them come to the surface, which causes an uncharacteristic outburst. Their insecurities can be an aspect of negative *chi* in the kidneys, the organ system of the Water Element. Water Monkeys are deeply private individuals, prone to secrecy, which can make others wary of them.

Water Monkeys swing through the trees of life always looking for new experiences – they hate dullness, routine and anything that forces them to be static – and they love a life that flows ever forward. Travel is one of their great passions. They may be impatient and indecisive, but Water Monkeys would do well to try to focus on a few single, important objectives, so as not to become deflected from their sense of purpose in life.

WOOD MONKEY: 1944, 2004
"Monkey in the Trees"

The spring-like energy of the Wood Element creates an even cleverer, sharper and more creative mind than is present in the other Monkey types, as well as enhancing the Monkey's intuition and perceptive ability. Wood also brings a greater interest in harmony and humanistic values than other Monkeys possess.

Wood has the effect of making this Monkey rather less mischievous than his or her Monkey cousins. Also, unlike other types, Wood Monkeys are charmingly diplomatic and skilled in negotiation. They possess good communication skills and have a better understanding of other people. Their appreciation of nature's harmony makes them more tolerant of others, so they can work well with others around them, becoming collaborative rather than meddling.

With their retentive mind and good sense of realism, Wood Monkeys are aware of what is going on generally and able to foretell outcomes. They're good at applying themselves to various tasks and being able to get things under control. They make wonderful pioneers, who are interested in new trends, prepared to overcome problems, and always want to achieve success. The downside of such a love of new ventures, though, is that they can suffer from believing that the "grass is greener" elsewhere, and may move on too quickly from one project to another.

At times touchy and oversensitive, a result of an imbalance of *chi* in the liver, the organ system of the Wood Element, Wood Monkeys can become overly concerned with detail and should instead learn to look at the bigger picture.

FIRE MONKEY: 1956, 2016
"Monkey Climbing the Mountain"

Irrepressibly sparky, the Fire Monkey is perpetually energized and impassioned. Self-confident and highly competitive, this Monkey is inventive, impetuous and imaginative, and has a very strong nerve.

Fire Monkeys are dominant and animalistic and will always take the initiative. Their egotistical, controlling and innovative natures have big effects on their surroundings. They're adventurous and audacious, constantly on the move, and ever-willing to take a risk – often without considering the consequences. Always wanting to get the better of people, and sometimes suspicious of others in ways that are not justified, they're often experienced as pushy and overbearing. Despite all that, Fire Monkeys love to have praise and appreciation heaped upon them – and they often are. Although their methods may be self-centred, they can make a lot of good things happen.

THE MONKEY 猴

When it comes to romance (if they can find time for it), Fire Monkeys are sensual, dominant and motivated – but they can also be prone to deep jealousy and can be changeable. Only a strong character will pin down a Fire Monkey.

Being unrealistic and rash is not the most effective way for any Monkey to enjoy life to the full. Fire Monkeys should try to slow down, take some rest, and consider a less single-minded approach to their plans. Then, they can ease the flow of *chi* through their heart and circulation (the organ system of the Fire Element) to enjoy greater emotional, spiritual and financial success overall.

EARTH MONKEY: 1908, 1968, 2028
"Lone Monkey"

The stabilizing Earth Element helps to moderate the irrational Monkey tendencies to create a more grounded, serious and level-headed type, who is a lot more conventional, contemplative, caring and compassionate than the others.

Less excitable than other Monkeys, and so less prone to distraction, Earth Monkeys can control their emotions, making them less nervy, impulsive and rash. Thinking, principled and knowledgeable individuals, Earth Monkeys like to follow the rules, but without lacking ingenuity. Unlike most of their clan, they're straightforward, dependable and honest. The most altruistic Monkey type, Earth Monkeys are genuinely concerned for others: they still have a strong sense of self, but they're simply not as self-centred as other Monkeys, keeping their egos under control. They're generous, liked and appreciated accordingly – and if they're not appreciated, they have the Monkey tendency to become upset about it.

In romance, Earth Monkeys are dependable and kind, but have a strong sense of independence, which means that any potential partner may have to be understanding of the Earth Monkey's need to pursue his or her own needs.

Not surprisingly, this Monkey type makes the most reliable progress toward achieving objectives in life. However, Earth Monkeys would be wise to put the rule book aside occasionally, so that they don't self-limit their considerable abilities. The stomach, spleen and pancreas are the organ system belonging to the Earth Element, meaning the Earth Monkey is well advised not to overindulge.

WORK, CAREER AND MONEY
Curious; Dextrous; Competitive; Resourceful; Strategic

THE MONKEY IN WORK AND CAREER

As Monkeys would say, it's a jungle out there! But, thankfully, Monkeys have a formidable array of skills to help them adapt to any workplace. They're quick to learn, good at finding and showing other people better ways to do things, and able to innovate ideas and implement them – and react quickly to changing circumstances. They're well-read, have technical expertise, and are extremely gifted communicators. What more could anyone ask for in an employee?

However, Monkeys can also be over-confident, which means they're not good at taking criticism, nor open to the advice of others. They lack empathy, understanding and respect for others, but may be glad to help as long as they're approached in the right way – with compliments.

Monkeys prefer to lead rather than be led, getting on best if they have an important role in a small to medium-sized company, rather than finding themselves lower down in a global corporation. With such an array of talents and survival skills, they can also make a great success of self-employment.

In general, Monkeys are preoccupied with the here and now and are not necessarily good at career planning. However, as consummate strategists, Monkeys should in theory be excellent at setting themselves targets and achieving them by any means necessary, so success is definitely firmly within their grasp.

COMMON CAREER POSSIBILITIES

• SALES • COMMUNICATIONS • ENGINEERING • FINANCE • ACTING •
• WRITING • TRADER • INVENTOR • DOCTOR • TEACHER • PERFORMER •
• SPECULATOR • PLANNER • LAWYER • SCIENTIST • SPORTSPERSON •

THE MONKEY

THE MONKEY AND MONEY

Monkeys have a reputation for being good at making money, good at spending it, generous toward friends with it – and consequently bad at saving it. With the Monkey, it's all in-the-moment stuff, with little forethought for times ahead that may be less financially secure. All that's probably a product of the fact that, with so much enterprise and imagination coursing through their veins, Monkeys find money relatively easy to come by.

Monkeys have good instincts for matters of finance – which, more than anything, is simply a facet of their complex and sophisticated array of self-preservation methods. They seem highly adept at gaining financial benefit from just about any set of circumstances or group of contacts – and their address books are full of contacts. Their keenly tuned money-seeking radar constantly bleeps with ventures that could make them wealthy, and its range is far-reaching.

Monkeys are particularly good at making instant assessments of any financial proposition, and accurately weighing up the likelihood of making gains – and then taking a gamble. Those watching them might also get lucky; but they might miss the fleeting, optimum moment that the Monkey is so good at catching. Unfortunately for the rest of us, the Monkey is unlikely to give away the secrets of his or her success (and anyway it's mostly down to instinct) – and to try to emulate the Monkey's methods merely sets the rest of us up for failure.

Monkeys are also great bargain-hunters (sometimes to the point of pettiness), haggling, conniving and doing whatever it takes to get the best price and the best rate of return. If the situation demands it, they may resort to unscrupulous methods for financial gain, too. They wouldn't stoop as low as actual crime, of course – they have no need, because their charm gives them such appeal that anyone on the receiving end of the Monkey's mischief will find themselves forgiving it, even if they really didn't intend to!

Monkeys are short-term speculators and this is where their skills hold most influence. It's best that they don't try to invest in long-term ventures, as they're not great with long-range foresight. They would do well to think about their own future now and then – perhaps saving some money for a rainy day.

PREFERENCES AND WELL-BEING
Lighting up the room

PEOPLE, TASTES AND PASTIMES

The Monkey is the most gregarious of the Chinese Zodiac signs. Monkeys simply love to be around lots of people as often as possible – and if they're not with them in person, they'll be on the phone, on a social networking site, or using any other possible channel of communication to keep in touch.

Monkeys love to light up a room, entertaining any gathering with their sparkling wit and nonstop conversation. They have lots of friends, from a variety of backgrounds and cultures – there's not a hint of judgmentalism or prejudice in the Monkey. Monkeys pick sets of friends to accompany them to different occasions and activities – they know that some friends may not be able to keep up with their endless action, while others may tire of their incessant chatter (the Monkey has opinions on everything and is always ready to share them).

These people have distinctly metropolitan tastes, having little or no time for the countryside. For Monkeys, rural life is simply too dull and too slow – and there aren't enough people around at all times of day and night for them to have fun with. With their love of being out and about and busy at all hours, a Monkey's home isn't as important to him or her as it is to other signs of the Zodiac. When they *are* at home, Monkeys fill their space with people, family, noise and activity as much as they can.

Smart and fashionable, Monkeys show their whimsical and capricious natures when it comes to what they wear, always wanting to keep on trend. And they're suckers for flattery – if you tell them they look great in that, they'll buy it.

Monkeys seek stimulation and excitement, day and night. They're hopeless at resisting temptation and can easily overindulge themselves in whatever new thrill is on offer, frequently getting themselves into trouble in the process – trouble that is almost invariably of their own making. At home, Monkeys enjoy absorbing activities, such as learning to play a musical instrument. And unsurprisingly, a Monkey's vacation has to be action-packed and brimming with lively and interesting people to chat to. Find a glamorous city with plenty of nightlife, and that's exactly where a Monkey will be.

HEALTH AND WELL-BEING
Fixed Element: Metal

Monkeys approach life bursting with positivity, they tackle issues head on and with energy and are proactive in getting on with their objectives. They don't sit around fretting and worrying – there isn't time. The result is that they're strong, healthy individuals, who can face and overcome health problems if they do occur.

However, it's not always as straightforward as that. With their ultra-high-speed lives, Monkeys can easily take too much out of themselves. Nonstop mental activity can make them subject to nervous disorders, although these may not be immediately evident – the Monkey is a master of exuding confidence, even if inside he or she feels anxious or insecure.

Anxiety and insecurity are the result when something is out of kilter. For example, if a Monkey's life is not stimulating enough, or if he or she is confined, excluded or otherwise alone for long periods of time, or if he or she is not getting enough attention, a deep unhappiness can lurk beneath the effervescent exterior. If Monkeys eat too much "on the hoof", rather than sitting down, resting and enjoying their food properly, they can also find themselves prone to nervous or digestive complaints.

The antidote to all this is not complicated, but it does require Monkeys to adopt uncharacteristic discipline. First, they are well advised to avoid hyperactivity by taking regular rests and breaks. They should try to give their minds a rest, by immersing themselves in regular physical exercise. They should take time to eat proper meals. And finally, they should open up to others when they feel down or dejected, rather than simply becoming bitter. In these ways they can free up the *chi* that flows through their lungs and respiration, the organ system of the Metal Element, and work themselves back to good health.

THE ROOSTER

ROOSTER YEARS: 1909, 1921, 1933, 1945, 1957, 1969, 1981, 1993, 2005, 2017, 2029
ROOSTER HOURS: 1700–1900
FIXED ELEMENT: METAL   YIN SIGN

With Metal as its fixed Element, the Rooster person is focused, direct, organized and meticulous. Whether dealing with finances, life or people, the Rooster will take charge, sorting everything and everybody into order.

Direct and outspoken, the Rooster is not slow to speak up, even sometimes coming across as blunt, bossy or critical. Unlikely to take advice or orders from others, the Rooster may appear interfering, often telling others what to do and how to live. This can sometimes make Roosters difficult for others to deal with, but despite appearances they only ever have our best interests at heart, wanting only to help other people and generally to make the world a better place.

Roosters enjoy being the centre of attention and in the spotlight, and are comfortable in social gatherings. Always smart and snappy in their dress, they have a proud stature and are happy to strut about and show off. Occasionally, though, this fanciful nature may spill over into conceit.

The Rooster also has a more vulnerable inner aspect, and he or she may become prone to anxiety. Stress, in turn, can make Roosters a little too picky, and they can get far too bogged down in their perfectionist natures.

The Rooster's complementary and opposite sign is the Monkey.

KEYWORDS
- EFFICIENT • PRECISE • HONEST • DIGNIFIED • PASSIONATE
- FLAMBOYANT • RELIABLE • FASTIDIOUS • HARDWORKING
- RESILIENT • ENTERTAINING • FUSSY • OUTSPOKEN • PERFECTIONIST

THE FIVE TYPES OF ROOSTER

METAL ROOSTER: 1921, 1981
"Rooster in a Cage"

Metal is the Rooster's fixed Element, so this person has double Metal influence, resulting in a Rooster with formidable mental powers and a virtually unflinching focus on structure and organization.

With their highly celebrated intellect, Metal Roosters have great capacity for analysis, investigation and deduction. However, to avoid extremes, they're advised that to rely wholeheartedly on mental analysis of a situation can limit their dedication to effective action and stunt their ability to pay proper attention to their own feelings and emotions. In other words, Metal Roosters need to make an effort to stop thinking sometimes and actually put their thoughts into practice, and to develop some emotional intelligence.

Extremely capable at managing and controlling others, Metal Roosters need also to remember that it's a virtue to be able to listen to others' points of view and perhaps even compromise their own beliefs in order to build stronger relationships. Paradoxically, establishing and valuing strong relationships with others enables Metal Roosters to make more of their own talents, rather than less. With their high ideals and strong work ethic, Metal Roosters are driven to improve their own circumstances *and* the circumstances of society.

Metal Roosters are good speakers. Their great, outspoken self-confidence makes them skilled at debate, although they are well advised to try not to appear self-important. They can enhance their immense capacity for enjoying life and for achieving success if they cultivate a little flexibility, diplomacy and gentleness – and if they make sure that they take time out for some fun, as they're prone to work too hard. The Metal Rooster should especially look after his or her lungs and respiration, the organ system of the Metal Element.

WATER ROOSTER: 1933, 1993
"Rooster in the Barnyard Pool"

The Water Element brings a calmer aspect and more intellectual depth to the Rooster prototype. Water Roosters are clear thinkers, who consider matters to their conclusion. They also have lots of energy.

This Rooster type possesses enviable logic and powers of concentration and focus. However, sometimes these attributes take over, giving Water Roosters a tendency toward excessive interest in the detail, and an almost obsessive perfectionism. In some situations, Water Roosters would do well to try to maintain a broader view of things so that they don't get bogged down and lose sight of the essentials. They're natural scientists, loving the minutiae of how things work and how things are done, and they may apply this interest to more cultural pursuits, too – for example, the technical aspects of a piece of music, or the particular brush strokes used in a work of art.

Like all Roosters, Water Roosters are great communicators, but they also benefit from water's ability to wend its way around obstacles. This makes them superb negotiators, able to persuade and influence others with consummate ease. Water Roosters are also adaptable and have good diplomatic skills; they're able to understand others' points of view. Water Roosters have a deeply embedded streak of practicality. They're able to think clearly and then turn their thoughts to action. They enjoy home, and are good home-makers, but they should remember to rest and avoid depleting the *chi* energy in their kidneys, bladder and urinary system, the organs of the Water Element.

WOOD ROOSTER: 1945, 2005
"Rooster Crowing at Dawn"

Wood Roosters are especially imaginative, creative, productive, and interested in beauty. This Rooster tends to be better at teamwork than others in its clan, generally being more considerate, well-intentioned, reliable and fair. A committed individual, the Wood Rooster is always interested in moving things forward – in his or her own life, but also in terms of being especially motivated to work for

THE TWELVE ANIMAL SIGNS

good causes and improve society in general. Wood Roosters are as optimistic and positive about other people as they are about themselves, which gives them a kind of naïvety when dealing with others. They can be unrealistic about how committed, capable and enthused others will be in helping them, assuming that everyone has the same energy for the cause as themselves. As a result, Wood Roosters can sometimes overcommit, creating situations in which, without the full support of others, things are just too complicated and unmanageable. It's important, therefore, that Wood Roosters don't take on too much.

Wood Roosters have a more open-minded nature than other Rooster types, making them more adaptable and more able to improvise if they're caught unawares. They're curious about life, and interested in learning. When it comes to communication, like all Roosters they speak directly, but they can be too quick to criticize – they should take care not to speak up too hastily. They have a special need to draw their family and close friends to them, expressing their affectionate natures. The Wood organs are the liver and gall bladder, so Wood Roosters should take care not to drink too much alcohol, or overindulge in rich foods.

FIRE ROOSTER: 1957, 2017
"Rooster on its Own"

The Fire Element creates a Rooster who is highly animated, dramatic and passionate. With his or her inflammatory disposition, the Fire Rooster goes about things with short-lived bursts of energy, and may focus too much on the superficial. Fire Roosters are highly dynamic and often brilliant, capable of quick changes of mood, action or strategy – in Chinese tradition, Fire Roosters are often compared to shooting stars.

Audaciously seeking success for themselves, Fire Roosters are prepared to take risks to get where they want to be. However, they're also capable in positions of authority. They have others' best interests at heart and are good at organizing. At the same time, they should beware of dominating others in order to pursue their own needs. These Roosters can lack empathy and flexibility and may have issues with trusting others to do the job properly, which means they may find it

THE ROOSTER 雞

difficult to delegate. On balance, though, as long as they try to even out their weaknesses, Fire Roosters have the potential to make great leaders. They have analytical natures and are particularly astute when it comes to matters of finance.

Fire Roosters are especially concerned with how others perceive them. They love praise and will groom and refine their appearance to attract it. Theatrical and temperamental, Fire Roosters need to remember to rein in their loud crows every now and then, so as not to appear impossibly attention-seeking. They're well advised to take care not to burn out, causing an imbalance in the *chi* energy flowing through their heart and circulation, the organ systems of Fire.

EARTH ROOSTER: 1909, 1969, 2029
"Rooster Pecking in the Fields"

The Earth Rooster is a quieter, and more focused, grounded and inward-looking Rooster type. Practical, realistic and private, Earth Roosters tend to be more cautious than others in their clan. Also unlike its Rooster cousins, the Earth Rooster isn't preoccupied with showiness or materialism, which means he or she isn't interested in accumulating things that are simply glamorous or expensive.

Earth Roosters tend to be thoughtful, observant and analytical. They're particularly good at gathering information, checking the detail, and then sorting out their discoveries and systemizing them into a logical order. Of course, these make for excellent business skills, particularly in the area of finance. Careful, responsible and hardworking, Earth Roosters set themselves high standards in order to better themselves. They also expect the same of others, and can be strict at enforcing their operating methods.

Earth Roosters communicate in an open and straightforward manner and lead by example. However, with their zealous natures, they can be rather too keen to convert others to their way of thinking. As a result they can appear stubborn and resistant to change. If Earth Roosters can cultivate a little flexibility and an open mind, they may ease rather than block the path to self-betterment. In order to maintain the balance of *chi* in the spleen, stomach and pancreas (the organs of the Earth Element), Earth Roosters should moderate their intake of sweet foods.

WORK, CAREER AND MONEY

Meticulous; Committed; Perfectionist; Decisive; Bossy

THE ROOSTER IN WORK AND CAREER

Roosters are diligent and determined. Highly motivated to follow their career path all the way to the top, they often have good prospects for promotion and will happily switch occupations to achieve their goals. Able to think in terms of both their short-term and their long-term objectives, they're persistent, committed and ambitious. Unafraid of hard work, they're good at dealing with the ups and downs of any job and at overcoming setbacks.

The Rooster's excellent powers of intellect and logic are extremely valuable in any career. Furthermore, Roosters are often keen to help and have a strong sense of service to others. Highly organized and not afraid to get their hands dirty, they'll happily sort out problems, even if these were caused by other people. In fact, working out detailed solutions and providing a strategy for applying them can be pure delight for a Rooster.

Roosters are well suited to being self-employed, as they're able to juggle a wide range of tasks and are most comfortable when they can work independently, making steady and careful progress at their own speed. They don't like to admit to mistakes, nor to receive criticism, and they don't respond well to pressure or orders from others. They like to be creative and imaginative in the way they deal with things.

COMMON CAREER POSSIBILITIES

• PUBLIC SPEAKING • ACCOUNTANCY • FASHION • PLANNING
• DEBT COLLECTOR • BANK MANAGER • SECRETARY • PERFORMER
• WRITER • SINGER • PRESENTER • MUSICIAN

In employment, they enjoy holding positions of authority and are extremely reliable, efficient and responsible – although any boss will need to set out clearly what he or she requires, as otherwise Roosters may do things their own way.

Roosters are not the world's greatest diplomats – they tell it how they see it, which can be difficult when they have to deal with sensitive colleagues. To function within an organization, therefore, they may need to rein in their irrepressible natures and unwavering self-belief – either by their own self-discipline or through sensitive management.

THE ROOSTER AND MONEY

The Rooster is completely at home in the world of financial and commercial matters, and has great expertise in this area, with a particular skill for managing detail. Roosters are honest and straightforward where money is concerned, and whether at home or at work they're happy doing the books, balancing incomings and outgoings, making sure budgets are set and kept to, and generally keeping order. These people cannot stand financial matters that have been left ignored or unresolved – in the Rooster's home there'll be no unpaid bills and no unsubmitted tax accounts.

Happily for those around them, Roosters are more than willing to spread the benefits of their financial skills, always giving advice to friends and family, and may volunteer to look after other people's money. Even unsolicited or unexpected advice is likely to be reliable, for Roosters are able to find favourable financial potential in the unlikeliest of situations. Paradoxically, however, the Rooster's own financial fortunes can be prone to ups and downs. While Roosters tend to be brilliant at accumulating wealth, not all of them are able to hold on to it. A Rooster's attitude toward money may turn him or her into one of two kinds of people. On the one hand, Roosters can be exceptionally generous, spreading around their wealth to their nearest and dearest and revelling in the warmth this gives them. On the other hand, Roosters can be frugal to the point of miserliness, hoarding rather than spending their money. Put simply, Roosters are either spenders or savers – but rarely anything in between.

PREFERENCES AND WELL-BEING
Shaking the tail feather

PEOPLE, TASTES AND PASTIMES

Just like the animal they're named after, Roosters are the early birds in life – getting up and getting busy at the crack of dawn. Active and energetic, they're intolerant of laziness in their friends and family. However, even once others are up and active, Roosters will not want help with their own tasks – they prefer to look after their affairs themselves.

Roosters are good in a crowd, and generally they make better talkers than listeners. They enjoy socializing and make fabulous hosts, who love any opportunity to throw a party and show off their excellent cooking skills and their brilliant dress sense.

Appearance and image are extremely important to the Rooster, who will spend his or her money on the most stylish clothes and the most striking fittings and adornments for his or her home. Roosters keep their beady eyes out for the latest fashion trends, and although some will opt for the more conservative styles, whatever they wear Roosters are usually meticulously presented. Before a party or a night out, it will often be the Rooster who spends longest getting ready, making sure he or she looks perfect in every way. As appearances are so important to them, Roosters may judge those around them, too, by what they wear or how well they look after themselves. Hygiene is important to Roosters; they don't like dirt, and in their altruistic way may be quite prepared to sort out someone else's mess when they have to.

Roosters enjoy all manner of cultural activities, particularly performances of music or dance, and the fine arts. Despite being named after a farmyard animal, Roosters prefer to vacation in urban settings, which enables them to indulge their penchant for good-quality stores. They do also like to get away from it all, to reconnect with nature and experience some outdoor pursuits.

HEALTH AND WELL-BEING
Fixed Element: Metal

The organs associated with the Metal Element are the lungs and large intestine. For the Rooster, therefore, these body parts tend to be inherently strong and healthy, unless they're adversely affected by an unhealthy lifestyle. Roosters love spicy and pungent foods, which are associated with the palate of all those born under the Metal Element. However, Roosters are prone to overindulgence, which means that they'll often eat these (and for that matter other) foods to excess. The resulting imbalance in *chi* flowing through their lungs and intestine might manifest not only in a physical illness, but also in sadness or depression.

Roosters tend to rise early, enjoy the outdoors, and be good at coping with physical hardship. This means that their physical health is inherently good, and Roosters (who can't abide lounging around) won't easily give in to ill-health. Roosters rarely take days off from work – they're simply too busy to be ill.

Psychologically, though, Roosters are natural worriers – it's part of their make-up. As a result, Roosters' illnesses tend to manifest from psychological rather than physical causes – their excessive sense of self-discipline, their perfectionism, and their inability to sit still for a moment. None of this is necessarily a problem, unless the worrying gets out of hand. When this happens, Roosters may experience extreme tension and nervousness, mood swings or other emotional problems. Or, they may be afflicted with illnesses with a nervous component, such as asthma or severe headaches. To prevent things from going that far, and no matter how much they may feel that they are just too busy to address health problems or take things easy, Roosters need to, first, recognize which sources of stress they've created for themselves (a shift in attitude can remove these sources) and, then, identify which are legitimately stressful situations over which they have little control. They can deal with any residual stress by, for example, taking up a practice such as yoga or meditation; or doing something physically demanding, such as long runs or cycle rides, to burn up some of that bubbling energy. Furthermore, Roosters are well advised not to associate with too many other nervous people.

THE DOG

DOG YEARS: 1910, 1922, 1934, 1946, 1958, 1970, 1982, 1994, 2006, 2018, 2030
DOG HOURS: 1900–2100
FIXED ELEMENT: EARTH   YANG SIGN

Those born under the influence of the Dog have all the characteristics we might expect from this animal: they make great guardians, they can be dogmatic and dogged in their approach to things, and very often (although not always) their bark is worse than their bite. Sociable and loyal, Dog people place great importance on "pack" ties. They are good team players and they value their family above all, becoming fiercely protective if anyone they love is threatened. Dogs have strong moral principles and firmly believe in achieving justice. They may not have innumerable friends, but those they do have really matter.

Dogs have a reputation for nosiness, but their sniffing around is usually good-natured. When threatened, Dogs do have fiery tempers, but their reactions abate as quickly as they surfaced, unless matters aren't rapidly sorted out – in which case a Dog will hold a grudge. When things go badly wrong, when situations prove beyond their control, when they feel overwhelmed, or even when they're just on their own too much, Dogs may become anxious, pessimistic or even cynical. They can be slow to change their mind once it's made up, and they can have a rather simplified, black-and-white approach to people and issues.

The dog's complementary and opposite animal is the Pig.

KEYWORDS
• FAIR • EMPATHETIC • COMMITTED • HONOURABLE • AFFECTIONATE
• PROTECTIVE • LOYAL • DIRECT • CHEERFUL • UNSELFISH • RESOURCEFUL
• ALERT • PUGNACIOUS • DEFENSIVE • SULKY • TERRITORIAL

THE FIVE TYPES OF DOG

METAL DOG: 1910, 1970, 2030
"Dog in the Temple"

In Tibetan culture, this Dog type is known as the "Iron Dog", which offers insight into just how tough he or she is. Organized, serious, self-confident and decisive, Metal Dogs are unflinching and unyielding in terms of both their mental strength and their discipline. They're also passionate and outspoken.

High standards and strict principles can make Metal Dogs appear inflexible, but it also makes them courageous, dedicated and intensely loyal, never backing down from a cause and following through with action, no matter how daunting the situation in which they find themselves or how fearsome the opposition.

Metal Dogs are always enthusiastic about new projects and will brim with ideas to put them into action. Mentally, they possess strong logic, which means they place great emphasis on planning and will happily sort through other people's problems for them, although they're inclined to be dogmatic about the conclusions they draw. More than ready to speak their minds, they can be prone to gossiping, but they're also, as a result, less likely to become sulky or introspective than other members of the Dog clan.

Metal Dogs make bad enemies. They don't like to see rules broken or laws infringed, and they can be extreme in their pursuit of justice and punishment, rarely showing mercy when they catch the culprits. At home, however, their protective quality shows itself in displays of the utmost affection.

A little more light-heartedness and fewer campaigns can help Metal Dogs strike a better balance in their lives, freeing up the *chi* in their lungs and respiration (the organ system of the Metal Element). They should try to let people sort out their own issues from time to time, and sometimes let up on reading from the rule book – a little laissez-faire can be a good thing.

WATER DOG: 1922, 1982
"Family Dog"

The Water Element offers contemplative, intuitive and reflective possibilities to this calmer, deeper and more placid Dog. Far more fluid, flexible and adaptable than the standard Dog type, the Water Dog is also less aggressive and less anxious.

Water Dogs have a reputation for being difficult to take in or to fool. Like watchdogs, they're highly observant, not only when it comes to situations, but when it comes to people, too. Intuitively able to understand and accommodate other people's points of view, they're tactful, diplomatic and tolerant (sometimes to the point of being taken advantage of). Their empathy and charm makes Water Dogs the most popular of the Dog clan, and they often have lots of friends, rather than the small social circle that is more usual for a Dog type.

This is a free-wheeling type of Dog, running fast and loose with money and pleasure, making him or her rather less dependable than others in the clan. Water Dogs are emotional, passionate and romantic – sometimes excessively so. They can love rather too many people, finding it hard to commit their heart to just one, especially as they don't really like to be tied down. Furthermore, despite their intuition, they aren't very good at judging others' romantic intentions.

Water Dogs could benefit sometimes from taking a stronger line when it comes to their own judgment, and letting other people get away with less, so that they improve their own stature and appear less easily influenced. In terms of health, the Water Dog should try regular detoxification to protect the health of their kidneys and urinary system, the organ system for the Water Element.

WOOD DOG: 1934, 1994
"Guard Dog"

Creative and imaginative, the Wood Dog seeks balance and stability – he or she is as prone as any Dog to nervousness and anxiety. Less independent and less self-confident than other Dogs, the Wood Dog is good at hiding his or her insecurities and keeping up a brave front, but generally feels safest within a group he or she knows well. Wood Dogs value the support and protection of others and are keen to co-operate with and please them. Their warmth, generosity, helpfulness and understanding mean that Wood Dogs are easy to get along with. However, they are well advised not to become too reliant on the approval or support of others – a little more self-reliance, and being prepared to take the risk of upsetting someone once in a while, can help them to reach their own objectives more readily. One to one, Wood Dogs are able to build solid, long-lasting relationships. These are loyal, loving partners for life.

Growth is a common theme for those born under the Wood Element, and for Dogs this means being keen to develop their imagination and creativity, as well as pursuing their goals in life. Wood Dogs are the most refined of all the canine types, loving anything to do with the arts, and being rather less materialistic than others in the clan. In personal development, they should take care to examine their choices thoroughly, as they can be prone to making rash decisions when a little more depth and understanding might bring better results. Finally, Wood Dogs should moderate their intake of alcohol and fatty foods in order to protect their liver and gall bladder, the organ system of the Wood Element.

FIRE DOG: 1946, 2006
"Sleeping Dog"
This is a Dog with boundless energy. He or she is bold and excitable, independent and courageous, confident and self-assured, and has an irrepressible will.

The Fire Dog is a natural leader. Charming, charismatic, outgoing and sociable, he or she will head up the pack, easily attracting others and inviting them to follow. Fire Dogs can have intense personal magnetism, making them virtually irresistible to the opposite sex, and they tend to be successful in their personal relationships. This talkative Dog enjoys partying and having a good time.

Pioneering activities, and new and exciting experiences and adventures, are the passions of the Fire Dog. With all this positive, gutsy energy, they have the potential to become highly successful, but they also remain faithful to the traditional Dog qualities of dependability and honesty. As a result they're not likely to be corrupted by their success, popularity or partying.

On the more negative side, Fire Dogs tend to resist doing anything against their will. They'll try to avoid confrontation, but are fierce if they feel attacked or if they need to defend one of their pack. They won't hang around on the edge of the action – if they threaten to bite, they're willing to go through with it. Enemies would do well to let this "sleeping dog" lie.

Fire Dogs can be restless and unsettled, prone to agitation and worry, which they're likely to bottle up. The counsel of older and wiser, trusted friends may help build their confidence, calm their nerves and restore peace to the *chi* that flows through their heart and circulation, the organ system of the Fire Element.

EARTH DOG: 1958, 2018
"Dog on the Mountain"

A quieter, less emotional Dog, the Earth Dog is a sensible and serious person. Earth is also the Dog's fixed Element, and the double helping makes Earth Dogs more able to live in the here and now, as well as steadier, surer and more hardworking than other types. Known for their wisdom, Earth Dogs can be great thinkers, weighing up the pros and cons of every situation. They have a reputation for being good at handling money. They're keen to improve themselves, steadily moving forward in life.

When relating to others, Earth Dogs speak plainly, but from the heart, and they can give good advice. They're good listeners and display kindness toward and understanding of other people's situations, inspiring others to love and respect them and to have confidence in their ideas. This faith is justified – Earth Dogs are so honest and idealistic that they're pretty much incorruptible. They're affectionate, but not sentimental.

Earth Dogs can be secretive and hesitant, a little too selfless, and a little too unrealistic. They would do well to try to make sure they drive their own lives forward. Spending time with more dynamic individuals can encourage them to rouse themselves into action and not get too bogged down in other people's business. Earth Dogs need to monitor their sugar intake so as not to upset the flow of *chi* in the stomach, spleen and pancreas, the organs of the Earth Element.

狗 | THE TWELVE ANIMAL SIGNS

WORK, CAREER AND MONEY

Eager; Responsible; Patient; Honest; Wise; Adaptable

THE DOG IN WORK AND CAREER

Dogs make both good employees and good leaders and, being pack animals, they're excellent team players, co-operating well with others. They tend to be very much appreciated where they work, first because they're reliable and diligent in the execution of their tasks; and second because they have a legendary willingness to go beyond the call of duty to help out their colleagues. Their presence has a generally beneficial effect on staff morale and spirit.

Honest, trustworthy and focused, they can be relied upon in positions of responsibility, such as working with money, or handling confidential information. Their open natures makes them good at building working relationships. They're good at listening and at assessing other people. They make perfect managers, because they don't crave power, so they can be genuinely objective and supportive toward those they lead. Their inherently altruistic and principled natures mean that they're generally not ruthless career builders.

However, don't expect a Dog to be undiscerning about the jobs he or she takes on. Dogs tend to want to have an exact job description, and know what is expected of them; and they'll be particularly interested in whatever aspects of the work create real value, or bring benefit to society or to disadvantaged groups. With these criteria fulfilled, and as long as the task doesn't involve large amounts

---

COMMON CAREER POSSIBILITIES

• COUNSELLING • SOCIAL WORK • TRAVEL • POLITICS • LAW • EDUCATION
• DOCTOR • ACCOUNTANT • BANKER • DESIGNER • DIPLOMAT • BUILDER
• SCIENTIST • CARE WORKER • POLICEMAN • CHARITY WORKER

of conflict or confrontation, Dogs can turn their hands to almost anything. Combative work can trigger the Dog's legendary anxiety or pessimism, making him or her altogether less effective at the task in hand.

THE DOG AND MONEY

Dog people are not terribly materialistic, or interested in money for its own sake; they don't crave a luxurious lifestyle, self-pampering or opulent surroundings; they aren't preoccupied with living it up; and they don't need to have vast amounts in reserve. Actually, they care more about people than about money and all they want is to have enough cash for their own security and that of their beloved family. They do a job primarily for the value it creates, rather than to get rich – during a job interview, asking about the salary is more likely to be an afterthought than the first question on their lips. Whereas some animals in the Zodiac will spend money if they need to cheer themselves up, the Dog is more likely to find an altruistic pursuit to make him- or herself feel better.

Generally speaking, though, Dogs are wise when it comes to financial matters, and on the whole – but not always – they're relatively careful about their spending. Most will be able to achieve regular, modest savings, perhaps putting something away each month for a rainy day. All Dogs tend to be better at guarding other people's financial interests and resources than their own, as they're astrologically programmed for dedicated selflessness. Their charitable nature means that their generosity can have a financial dimension, although this is most often toward members of their pack, such as family or very close friends – but they're also likely to make donations to causes they deem worthy.

As with other aspects of life, Dogs have high moral ideals about money, and they're appalled by financial wrong-doing, against which they might well launch a campaign. Their exceptional nose for sniffing out what's going on and who's responsible means that perpetrators are likely to be called to account – and like a dog with a bone, the Dog person will not relent until he or she sees justice prevail. However, Dogs pry at their own peril: any unwelcome discoveries can bring on their characteristic gloom, which they may not shake for a rather long time.

PREFERENCES AND WELL-BEING

Watching, learning and interacting

PEOPLE, TASTES AND PASTIMES

First and foremost, Dogs like to be part of a "pack" – their companions are of crucial importance to them. One of the key characteristics of the Dog archetype is the ability to accept that people are unpredictable. This makes Dogs resilient and stable friends, generally unfazed by the challenges that relationships might bring. They're steadfast in their fidelity toward others and they have a moral determination to always "do the right thing" when dealing with others' circumstances – although this can make them indecisive.

While Dogs are not party animals, they do love to watch other people in social situations. In doing so, they learn to recognize patterns in people's behaviour and they try to fit in by imitating these patterns themselves. This can lead Dogs to accumulate a variety of important life skills. Dogs are also always looking to ascertain whether someone is an enemy or a friend, a member of the pack or an outsider, trustworthy or unreliable. Occasionally, the simplistic nature of the conclusions they draw can send Dogs off course, unfairly pigeon-holing other people. And, if you upset a Dog, he or she may become angry – but the anger will readily subside and the Dog is unlikely to make the attack personal.

Dogs are far too serious to succumb to frivolous trends. They can't engage in the trivial nature of fashion. On vacation, when they aren't watching the world go by, they'll immerse themselves in local customs and try to uncover the distinctive character of the place they're in – whether that's urban or rural is equally pleasant to the Dog. It will, however, be somewhere the entire family wants to go – Dogs are too consultative to pick somewhere without it having been agreed by the pack. Generally, they love travelling, and are happy to interrupt their travel to stop at unusual or unexpected places, taking in the local atmosphere with their customary canine inquisitiveness.

Studying customs may well feature in their hobbies, too. Mostly, however, Dogs like to spend their spare time indulging in active pursuits, such as gardening, or exploring the countryside with their proverbial nose to the ground.

HEALTH AND WELL-BEING
Fixed Element: Earth
Tough and resilient, Dogs have strong constitutions, giving them basically excellent underlying health. They're philosophical about times of difficulty, making it easy for them to cope with challenges. They tend to approach adversity that would disturb or stress others with their characteristic positive attitude and they have an innate ability to achieve basic, simple happiness.

Confusingly, given their ability to overcome true hardship, they can often feel anxious without real cause. When they get nervous about something, their fretting, pessimistic nature comes to the fore, perhaps leading to problems such as eczema or acne or other stress-related skin conditions. Dogs are able to express their emotions, but they're reluctant to go to the doctor, so they may ignore physical symptoms of illness for a long time. The organ system of the Dog's Fixed Element of Earth is the stomach and digestive system, which means that Dogs, who are completely unfussy when it comes to what they eat, should moderate their intake of sugar and rich, fatty foods.

Dogs tend to stay active well into old age. In their twilight years, they seem to maintain the spirit of youth, constantly giving back to society without any sign of age slowing them down. They can, however, be prone to arthritis, so all Dogs should try to take regular exercise, especially if they have a sedentary job.

The most important ingredient for the Dog's good health is the beneficial energy of the pack. Without their family and friends, Dogs can become lethargic or melancholy. They need stimulation from company, the collective experience of working together, and the security of a loving relationship. A tight schedule, imposed by someone else, may also cause gloom to descend upon a Dog. To lift their mood, Dogs need plenty of aerobic, endorphin-inducing exercise, such as swimming or dancing, and the fresh air of the countryside.

THE PIG

PIG YEARS: 1911, 1923, 1935, 1947, 1959, 1971, 1983, 1995, 2007, 2019, 2031
PIG HOURS: 2100–2300
FIXED ELEMENT: WATER   YIN SIGN

Those born under the sign of the Pig are fastidious and sophisticated. They love their creature comforts. The Pig's home is his or her castle – it may not be tidy, but it will be a gorgeous place where the Pig can guard his or her privacy closely.

Pigs are extremely hardworking, making sure their family has all the basic necessities of life (and a few luxuries, too). They never want to bring their work home, though, making clear distinctions between home and family life, keeping home a place where everyone can be at ease. They're excellent at sticking at a job until it's completed. In fact, they're the embodiment of the idiom "pig-headed", meaning extremely stubborn. They enjoy pleasure, luxury and pampering – sometimes spending too long and too much on making themselves look and feel great when they should really be doing other things.

Pigs are eager to please and keen to help others. They can be trusting to the point of naïvety, which means that others may exploit them, or at least take them for granted. They do not like disharmony and will go out of their way to avoid confrontation. Paradoxically, they also have the wild boar's capacity to be extremely dangerous when cornered or when they feel deeply wronged.

The Pig's complementary and opposite sign is the Dog.

KEYWORDS

• KIND • HONEST • PATIENT • GENEROUS • ENDURING
• HUMOROUS • LOYAL • FUN • SENSUAL • SOCIABLE • INDUSTRIOUS
• TENACIOUS • STUBBORN • SIMPLE • INNOCENT • DANGEROUS • NAÏVE

THE FIVE TYPES OF PIG

METAL PIG: 1911, 1971, 2031
"Pig in the Garden"

The Metal Element brings structure to the Pig's personality, so that Metal Pigs are assertive, committed and strong, particularly when faced with challenges. More dominant, proud and intensely passionate than other Pigs, Metal Pigs work hard to achieve their aims. And when they make decisions, they tend to stick to them.

Metal Pigs are more likely to be satisfied by their work than to be exhausted by it. Their enthusiasm generates big ideas and strong opinions that they're happy to voice. They'll work as hard for others as they do for themselves, and will fight for justice and against prejudice or unfairness. Others consider them utterly dependable and this reputation is of great significance to them.

Simplistic in nature, Metal Pigs can take a rather black-and-white view of the world. Combined with the direct and forceful ways in which they communicate (they express their emotions vociferously), this can make them lacking in subtlety. Metal Pigs make formidable opponents because they're not only extremely tough, but also extremely bad losers. Their perseverance and endurance is legendary – these Pigs simply will not give up, so oppose them at your peril.

Metal Pigs invest a lot of their time and energy in building strong relationships, and are particularly intent on securing a firm family life that closely guards the welfare of their children. On the one hand, they have the natural Pig tendency to be overly trusting and optimistic about other people, but on the other, Metal Pigs can be insecure about others, becoming clingy or jealous when they sense lack of commitment. Metal Pigs function best in a stable relationship.

Metal Pigs are well advised to lighten up about life and keep a sense of humour in times of difficulty. In these ways, they can maintain the smooth flow of *chi* in the lungs and respiratory system, the organ system of the Metal Element.

THE PIG 豬

WATER PIG: 1923, 1983
"Pig in the Forest"

The Water Pig provides a double helping of Water Element and is the last sign in the complete 60-year cycle. Deeply composed, perceptive, persuasive and sentimental, Water Pigs are the most emotionally intelligent among the Pig clan.

Water Pigs are good at seeing deep inside people. They can form close relationships and, like all the Pig types, can be loving and passionate. Their sympathetic, understanding, helpful and kind natures mean they believe in good causes and are always ready to help. They're diplomatic and good at negotiation and would rather find a peaceful solution to any problems than engage in combat. If things go too far, however, like all Pigs they can make formidable enemies. Generally, though, it's their softer side that they put on show. In fact, it's possible for Water Pigs to be overly soft-hearted, too often seeing the best in people, which gives others the opportunity to take advantage of them.

Although they're sociable, enjoying being around people, Water Pigs are not the most confident of the clan, and are happiest of all when at home with their loved ones. They reach their greatest potential when in a profound relationship.

This Pig is industrious, purposeful and honest. He or she is good at business in a way that is less showy than some of the other Pigs, and they're good at saving, too. Their naturally limiting nature means that Water Pigs are not generally prone to excess. However, if the balance of their *chi* energy is upset – particularly as it flows through the kidneys and urinary system – they can suffer from nervous complaints or overindulge in food, drink or luxury.

WOOD PIG: 1935, 1995
"Pig Passing By"

The Wood Element draws out the Pig's more subtle qualities of humour and optimism, so that this Pig has the wonderful ability to spread good cheer. The Wood Element governs the liver and gall bladder, and healthy Wood *chi* brings lightness and a capacity for growth. However, when that *chi* is out of balance, the Wood Pig may become angry, impatient or controlling.

THE TWELVE ANIMAL SIGNS

Hardworking and practical, the Wood Pig is good at securing financial funding and understands how to develop his or her career successfully. Although Wood Pigs are ill at ease with bureaucracy, they're very good at making influential connections by constantly being the people to help others with their problems. Generous with their time and money, they put a great deal of effort into good charitable causes, helping to raise awareness of them.

Although shy like others in the Pig clan, these Pigs are diplomatic and persuasive, and handle people well. This is because they have a natural ability to empathize with others. They like to work collaboratively and co-operatively, and so are able to build partnerships and alliances. Wood Pigs are team players, who don't go in for hierarchy. However, sometimes their wish to meet everyone on a level playing field can mean they're not discriminating enough about the company they keep – and this can affect both their reputation and their fortunes. They can also be somewhat manipulative, but usually without any malicious intent.

The Wood Pig's top priority – perhaps even his or her reason for living – is to be at home with the family. It's for this that the Wood Pig makes every effort to have a successful career. All Wood Pigs also need to have regular contact with nature, through such activities as weekend walks in the countryside.

FIRE PIG: 1947, 2007
"Pig Crossing the Mountain"

The Fire Pig is the most intense of all the Pig types. Fire Pigs are full of emotional energy, they have a bold, adventurous spirit, and they're impulsive and assertive. The Fire Pig may be a person who is more opinionated, more confrontational and generally more extreme than the rest of the Pig clan.

This self-confident Pig seems to be undaunted by a challenge and refuses to be discouraged in the pursuit of his or her goals. Courageous, audacious and even heroic, Fire Pigs are willing to take risks even if they're not strictly necessary. In their quest for new experiences, Fire Pigs are prepared to have a go at anything – being mediocre simply does not fit with their spontaneous and rash natures. The outcomes of such bold adventures are virtually unpredictable.

Although prone to selfishness, Fire Pigs often choose to support good causes in lavishly demonstrative ways and showing generosity of heroic proportions. They can be good leaders and good employers, but will become stubborn to the point of being irresponsible if things go badly.

Fire Pigs love pleasure and luxury, preferring nothing more than to support their family in style – although they'll spend less time wallowing in comfort at home than others in the clan. Love and romance are big motivators for them.

In general, they need to control the more extreme aspects of their energies to maintain a measure of emotional stability. The Fire Element governs the heart and circulation, and for the benefit of these systems the Fire Pig should beware of the health implications resulting from their attraction to danger.

EARTH PIG: 1959, 2019
"Pig in the Monastery"

The Earth Pig is the gentlest of the Pig clan. Patient, practical and reliable, this Pig has a solid disposition; he or she is less likely to get carried away with life than other Pig types.

Earth Pigs are methodical and organized. Financially shrewd, they're known for planning well for the future. They tend to be realistic in their goals and make good employers – preferring to lead by example rather than command – and good business partners. They seek a peaceful life in which to make their steady, quiet and generally unruffled progress toward success. Earth Pigs are not particularly prone to stress or worry, and can put up with difficulties and challenges that would throw many other people off the rails.

Like all Pigs, Earth Pigs love the home, and are liable to be content with their family and home life. All the same, they're certainly not without passion. They enjoy socializing and make loyal friends. They also love food and drink. The Earth Element governs the organ system of the stomach, spleen and pancreas, so, if Earth Pigs overindulge they can easily put on too much weight and become lethargic. In order to maintain their steady natures, Earth Pigs should avoid sugar highs and lows, as the Earth Element handles the body's blood-sugar levels, too.

THE TWELVE ANIMAL SIGNS

WORK, CAREER AND MONEY
Creative; Methodical; Resolute; Patient; Practical

THE PIG IN WORK AND CAREER

Pigs are well suited to all manner of occupations, but they may particularly enjoy work that has a practical or physical aspect. They also enjoy learning and study. Undaunted by a challenge or adversity, they're happy to apply themselves to a task with complete commitment, working hard, getting on with the job in hand, and using all their skills and abilities.

Pigs are known for paying close attention to detail and having a naturally high standard of workmanship. They don't rush at the jobs they're doing or jump ahead of themselves – and they'll certainly avoid taking risks. Instead, they like to progress methodically, step by step, and concentrate on one thing at a time. Tending to live in the here and now, Pigs are not adept at long-term planning, nor are they overly ambitious – they don't crave power for its own sake, and they probably wouldn't even think about advancing themselves by backstabbing or climbing over other people.

Good organizers and managers, with excellent all-round "people skills", Pigs have a natural ability to bring groups together, relishing contact with others over the course of their working day. They enjoy working co-operatively and are good team players. They're generally popular among their peers at work, and easy for managers to handle, as long as they're not asked to do something they're not

---

COMMON CAREER POSSIBILITIES

• TEACHING • CRAFTS • MEDICINE • WRITING • LAW • MUSIC
• SOCIAL WORK • CATERER • ARTIST • ENTERTAINER • DESIGNER
• FUNDRAISER • VETERINARIAN • FLORIST • HUMAN RESOURCES

confident they'll get right. With their adaptability, diverse skills set and self-motivation, they can also function very well in self-employment.

Charity work offers a particularly suitable career route for Pig people. Pigs like to do work that creates value for others, whether that's by fundraising for a large charitable organization or helping colleagues with their own work, for example, in a role in human resources or training.

If Pigs are asked to move out of their comfort zones, perhaps being asked to work faster, or do things in a way that isn't really their style, they can become stressed and anxious in the workplace. It's also really important to Pigs that they have good work–life balance, with a job that allows them to switch off at the end of the working day and go and enjoy their time at home, pottering around the house or enjoying some leisure time with those closest to them.

THE PIG AND MONEY

Pig types seem to enjoy shopping and spending money – both on themselves and for the benefit of their family, friends and partners. They're known for their generosity and they enjoy giving and also helping people out financially. They may make charitable donations, but they're most likely to spend money on something that affords them comfort and luxury, particularly in their home. They also like to celebrate life by indulging their love of socializing.

Pigs have a taste for the best in everything – not because they're snobbish about labels or because they're particularly sophisticated, but because they're good at distinguishing between good and bad quality, and they derive a lot of pleasure out of having gorgeous things. They see the sense in having the best they can afford, rather than always opting for a bargain.

Despite their love of spending, Pigs are wise with money, and good at seeking it out. When they need money, they have a reputation for finding it right under everyone's noses, where no one else could – rather like their animal counterpart snuffling out truffles in the woods. However, because they don't naturally consider the long term, Pigs are well advised to make a conscious effort to make allowances for "rainy days", and try to save some of what they earn.

| THE TWELVE ANIMAL SIGNS

PREFERENCES AND WELL-BEING
Indulging the senses

PEOPLE, TASTES AND PASTIMES

Pigs are notoriously gregarious, easygoing and extrovert, and they enjoy the company of other people. Happily, they're also easy people for others to be with: they're well-liked and popular and have a wide circle of friends. Entertaining to be around, Pigs are good at rising to the occasion of a party or other gathering, putting on their widest smile and most charming air. In their own homes, Pigs enjoy hosting parties and cooking for guests, offering excellent hospitality with plenty of good food and wine. Pigs are people who believe in sharing – both what is theirs and what's yours!

The Pig's easygoing nature means he or she can form relationships that, perhaps over time, become imbalanced. Pigs have a naturally generous attitude toward their friends and they often find it difficult to say no, which results in a high tolerance for people taking them for granted. However, when others' attitudes toward their generosity become too obviously exploitative, Pigs may lose their temper. Their endless wish to see the best in people can mean they feel a deep sense of betrayal if they're treated badly or deceived in any way.

Pig types are connoisseurs of sensual pleasure. They love to experience cultural and gastronomic delights – to the point of excess. They'll readily invite their friends into their homes, which are the most important places in their lives. A Pig may not keep his or her home immaculate (there simply isn't time for that), but it will always be clean, comfortable, welcoming and beautiful, and visitors will feel instantly at ease there.

Pigs work extremely hard. To balance this, it's important that they spend quality time on vacation, preferably with those closest to them. Taking it easy, with good food, drink and company, is just about the perfect way for a Pig to unwind from daily life.

However, the Pig's weakness for overindulging is especially tested during time off from routine. When they're on vacation or simply taking time out, Pigs can benefit greatly from self-control in order to make quite sure they don't descend into a quagmire of excess, profligacy or even depravity.

HEALTH AND WELL-BEING
Fixed Element: Water
The Water Element influences the health and well-being of the Pig via the organ system of the kidneys, bladder and urinary system, which also has effects on the reproductive organs. Staying up too late or overworking and getting run down depletes the *chi* energy of the kidneys, having deleterious effects on the Pig's all-round, long-term health.

However, day to day, Pigs have a robust constitution, quite literally fed by their tremendous appetite. Despite this innate strength, Pigs often believe they're fragile. Prone to anxiety, a Pig can be something of a hypochondriac. The excessive worry caused by hypochondria – regardless of the fact that the Pig has probably imagined his or her ill-health – can lead to problems with the stomach and other digestive organs, including acidity or stomach ulcers. Pigs who feel ill, even if it's in their heads, will feel sorry for themselves and will need to be mollycoddled in order to bring on "recovery". Of course, too much inertia as a result of illness – real or imagined – can have its own health implications, particularly weight gain and especially during middle age.

To ensure good health, Pigs need to make sure they participate in physical activity on a regular basis. Avoiding excess and having a regular exercise routine are essential. Pigs must also try to get out into nature as much as possible, and take up creative or cultural activities to stimulate their minds. Making sure they don't work too hard, spending time in company and ensuring they make time for dedicated, quality relaxation (rather than just lethargy) are important, too. Finally, Pigs should take care not to suppress their emotions; instead they should express their feelings freely to those closest to them so they don't become frustrated, and then explode in an infrequent, but characteristic, temper.

CHAPTER TWO

RELATIONSHIPS AND COMPATIBILITY

Traditional Chinese astrology considers relationships probably the most important application of astrological studies. For ordinary people in rural communities, knowing about the prospects for couples in marriage was a pragmatic exercise aimed at giving love – and childbearing – the best chance of success. In this chapter you'll find individual assessments of the general relationship qualities for each animal sign, together with a brief assessment of their partnership potential with someone of the same sign and with each of the 11 other signs in the cycle. The chief determinant in using the information in this chapter is the animal sign for your year of birth. However, the signs for your month and hour of birth, and the mutable Element for your year of birth, can add significant moderating influences on compatibility.

RELATIONSHIPS AND COMPATIBILITY

FACTORS IN COMPATIBILITY

For the Chinese, the Circle of Compatibility (below) and the Circle of Conflict (opposite) provide the best overall indication of how well two signs will get along with one another. The Circle of Compatibility is made of up four Triangles of Affinity. The three signs connected by each triangle represent the most favourable combinations. So, for example, one Triangle of Affinity connects the Horse, Tiger and Dog, meaning that a relationship between any two of these three signs has the greatest chance of success in that circle. The most unfavourable combination for any sign is with its opposite sign on the Circle of Conflict. For the Horse, for example, this is the Rat. Beyond these two circles, a sign in a relationship with its paired animal (see Chapter One) also presents a favourable combination, while

THE CIRCLE OF COMPATIBILITY

FACTORS IN COMPATIBILITY

THE CIRCLE OF CONFLICT

all the remaining combinations offer variable degrees of likely success. For each pairing listed in this chapter, a score out of ten represents that pairing's potential compatibility – although bear in mind this is a notional guide only.

MAKING THE MOST OF RELATIONSHIP POTENTIAL

It's important to remember that relationships are not guaranteed success or doomed to failure purely through astrological compatibility. These assessments can only guide us on how we might improve our understanding of another person in order to take steps to help the relationship fulfil its potential.

Normal human factors in forming relationships apply. A supposedly "ideal" combination does not produce an ideal relationship if the two people are not respectful of one another; and a seemingly challenging partnership may function well if both parties are prepared to work at making it a success. Communication, commitment, trust and compromise are all characteristics needed to make a relationship work. They highlight the fact that astrology can only light the way – relationships are in the end what we make of them.

RELATIONSHIPS AND COMPATIBILITY

THE RAT IN RELATIONSHIPS

Attractive; Appealing; Extroverted; Charming; Magnetic

Gregarious and flirtatious, Rat people are extremely attractive to other people. They have a romantic, passionate and sensual disposition, and love to go on dates. They can be particularly excited by the early stages of a new relationship, and will want to ensure that there's still plenty of variety as it progresses. A Rat's partner needs to be able to keep up with the fast pace of the Rat's life, and show full commitment – even if the Rat seems to be secretive or withholding something.

PATTERNS OF COMPATIBILITY AND CONFLICT

The Rat is most compatible with the Dragon and the Monkey. These three are all highly active and creative people, with a similarly energetic outlook on life. The Horse is the Rat's diametrical opposite and the least compatible sign in the cycle.

THE RAT IN RELATIONSHIPS

The Rat in a relationship with the …

- **Rat: 6**

    As long as two Rats share common objectives and try not to outdo one another, there's good potential for success here – although more so in a business than in romance. The key to happy romance will be to ensure that each partner talks through any resentments, rather than letting them fester.

- **Ox: 7**

    The Rat and the Ox are paired animals in the cycle of signs, making this a combination that balances the Rat's yang energy with the Ox's yin. However, both people may want to have high levels of independence to pursue their own goals, which can become a stumbling block to lasting love.

- **Tiger: 6**

    The Tiger and the Rat both like to get their own way, which means that success in this relationship can require both individuals to learn to compromise when disagreements crop up. All in all, this pairing may in the end make a longer-lasting friendship than a full-scale romantic relationship.

- **Rabbit: 5**

    This combination makes a wonderful friendship, but the Rabbit and the Rat may be too different to become promising lovers. They both appreciate security, but the unpredictable and restless nature of the Rat may prove too unsettling for the cautious, peace-loving Rabbit.

- **Dragon: 10**

    A fantastic combination! The Rat and the Dragon show great mutual understanding, without threatening one another. There's plenty of excitement and passion, but each also allows the other some space. With the Dragon's drive and the Rat's opportunism, this pairing can achieve great things.

- **Snake: 7**

    There's scope here for a successful romance, as long as both the Snake and the Rat acknowledge and respect each other's differences and try to develop mutual understanding. In the long term, both will need to deal with issues as soon as they arise and make sure they work at keeping their relationship alive.

RELATIONSHIPS AND COMPATIBILITY

❈ Horse: 1

On the face of it, the Horse and the Rat appear to have much in common. At first, there may be mutual infatuation, but in fact these two want very different things and the relationship will tend to be characterized by conflict. It could take considerable hard work for this partnership to stand the test of time.

❈ Sheep: 3

This challenging combination presents two very different attitudes to life and styles of self-expression. To make the partnership work, the Sheep needs to be more focused and organized, and the Rat more tolerant and appreciative. Both would do well to develop a more caring attitude toward how the other feels.

❈ Monkey: 10

The Monkey and the Rat have similar outlooks on life and display plenty of mutual respect and understanding. There's also mutual attraction and a shared need for excitement. As long as they remember to talk things through when they need to, this relationship has every possibility for long-lasting happiness.

❈ Rooster: 4

Their competitive natures mean that the Rat and the Rooster present a conflicting combination. With time and effort from both, each might come to appreciate the other's qualities and ability to make a positive contribution to the relationship, but probably more successfully in business than in romance.

❈ Dog: 7

Despite their different interests, the Rat and the Dog know that they each bring something beneficial to a relationship, giving this pairing good potential for harmony. Fireworks and passion are unlikely, but there'll be a stable bond that with good communication can create long-term harmony.

❈ Pig: 7

There's plenty of excitement and attraction in this promising combination, which has good potential for a loving relationship that works in terms of companionship as well as romance. In order for it to go the distance, however, the Rat will need to acknowledge and respect the Pig's need for stability.

THE OX IN RELATIONSHIPS

Cautious; Loving; Supportive; Vulnerable; Dedicated

Although the Ox may be slow to commit, once the relationship is established, he or she will show utter constancy, expecting the same from a partner. Loving and gentle, the Ox wants to fully intertwine his or her life with another's, and can be easily hurt by any perceived deceit or betrayal. In order not to appear inflexible, Oxen are well advised to try to spark off a spirit of adventure in their relationships, and become more willing to try out new experiences.

PATTERNS OF COMPATIBILITY AND CONFLICT

The Ox is most compatible with the Snake and the Rooster. These three are all dedicated and determined people, who like to think things through. The Sheep is the Ox's diametrical opposite and the least compatible sign in the cycle.

The Ox in a relationship with the …

❋ **Ox: 5**

Although two Oxen show good understanding of one another's need for security and stability, their relationship is almost too comfortable – there's insufficient spark for long-lasting romance. To make the partnership work, both would need to become more adventurous and risk-taking.

❋ **Tiger: 4**

Attracted by their differences, at first these two seem to complement each other. However, before long the Ox and the Tiger will clash. The Tiger loves freedom and adventure, while the Ox wants security and quietue. Tuning in to each other's wavelengths in the long term will take enormous effort.

❋ **Rabbit: 7**

The Ox and the Rabbit both have qualities that complement each other to create a workable and contented romantic relationship. It may, however, appear a little dull (and makes for an undynamic business relationship), as neither wants to upset the status quo, take risks or go after thrills.

❋ **Dragon: 8**

This strong relationship is built on mutual attraction and admiration. Both the Ox and the Dragon are prepared to commit to each other and will work hard at achieving long-lasting harmony – despite their naturally unyielding natures. The Dragon is well advised to take account of the Ox's conservatism.

❋ **Snake: 10**

The Ox and the Snake share their world-view. They're both caring and home-loving, putting their family above all. Neither looks for a wild or thrilling social life, instead being content to enjoy simple pleasures together. The Snake needs to be careful not to take advantage of the more naïve Ox.

❋ **Horse: 4**

Only mildly compatible, the Ox and the Horse do not show great prospects for a successful long-term relationship. The Horse is independent, restless and driven, while the Ox is slow, intellectual and reflective. The relationship can work only if there's sustained flexibility and tolerance from both partners.

THE OX IN RELATIONSHIPS 牛

❀ Sheep: 1
There is simply no connection between the Ox and the Sheep – romantically or mentally. As neither of these people is terribly outspoken, there's likely to be conflict and unexpressed resentment, and very little excitement. The Ox may find the Sheep frivolous, and the Sheep may think the Ox uncivilized.

❀ Monkey: 6
Although it's likely to work better in business than in love, this is a reasonably compatible combination. The Ox and the Monkey may find it difficult to understand each other's way of life, and may have to work hard to appreciate their differences, but if they're able to build trust, there's potential for fun.

❀ Rooster: 10
A harmonious combination that shows love, passion and respect on both sides, the Ox and the Rooster share similar values – both dedicate themselves to getting a job done and both believe in the importance of authority and orderliness. Overall, there's wonderful potential for long-lasting happiness.

❀ Dog: 5
The Ox and the Dog show little attraction or empathy, and have little in common – they're simply ill at ease with one another. To make the relationship work romantically, both parties would need to share similar life goals, but as a campaigning partnership, there's potential for success.

❀ Pig: 8
The Pig has the potential to bring out a sense of adventure in the Ox, which is just what the Ox needs. There is mutual attraction and a potential for deep friendship, so this relationship shows great promise. Both may need to be prepared to keep working through any differences as they arise.

❀ Rat: 7
The Rat and the Ox are paired animals in the cycle of signs, making this a combination that balances the Rat's yang energy with the Ox's yin. However, both people may want to have high levels of independence to pursue their own goals, which can become a stumbling block to lasting love.

| RELATIONSHIPS AND COMPATIBILITY

THE TIGER IN RELATIONSHIPS

Adventurous; Impulsive; Independent; Romantic; Changeable

Dynamic, energetic and impulsive, Tigers need flexible and patient partners who won't endlessly want to tie them down. Although Tigers can appear to be loners, beneath the surface their feelings are intense and they're known for their romantic spirit and ardent sexuality. Unfortunately, however, they do also have a reputation for lack of faithfulness and even promiscuity. Despite their courageous personalities, Tigers may become insecure, craving emotional support.

PATTERNS OF COMPATIBILITY AND CONFLICT

The Tiger is most compatible with the Dog and the Horse. These are all strong communicators, who are straightforward, impulsive and outgoing. The Monkey is the Tiger's diametrical opposite and the least compatible sign in the cycle.

THE TIGER IN RELATIONSHIPS 虎

The Tiger in a relationship with the …

✤ **TIGER: 6**

A Tiger with a Tiger provides plenty of lust, fireworks and fighting. To make the relationship work, each needs to temper their will to dominate, striving instead to treat the other as an equal, although neither is good at compromise. They should also make an effort to suppress their loner tendencies.

✤ **RABBIT: 6**

A Rabbit with a Tiger shows potential for a workable combination, as long as each accepts the other's different communication style. The Rabbit's intuitive approach to life can help solve problems in the relationship, but the Tiger can make a meal of the Rabbit if the Rabbit doesn't know where he or she stands.

✤ **DRAGON: 8**

A dynamic and dramatic combination of personalities, the Dragon and the Tiger make a strong team with a deep attraction that's all claws, excitement and passion. However, both parties may want to be in charge, so for long-lasting harmony they'll need to work out who will be the one to compromise.

✤ **SNAKE: 3**

The Tiger may well be drawn to the Snake, but their different approaches to life and lack of natural empathy make it difficult for these two to trust each other. Moreover, neither is likely to be able to persuade the other to his or her point of view, further reducing their chances of achieving long-term harmony.

✤ **HORSE: 10**

What adventures the Horse and the Tiger can have! Both take a positive approach to life, and share their need for excitement and new experiences. A relationship between these two is likely to be characterized by loyalty and respect – and that goes for professional relationships between them, too.

✤ **SHEEP: 5**

The Sheep may provide a stabilizing influence on the Tiger, and the Tiger can look after the Sheep, but ultimately the Tiger will get bored with having to tread so carefully. Although the relationship may work as a business partnership, for long-term romance the Tiger needs more adventure.

RELATIONSHIPS AND COMPATIBILITY

❈ Monkey: 1

The Tiger's fixed Element of Wood conflicts with the Monkey's Metal, so although opposites may initially attract, in the long term it's unlikely that these two will understand one another. They're also both highly competitive; it would take a great deal of compromise for the relationship to work.

❈ Rooster: 6

Two attention-seekers in the same relationship can lead to competition, making the relationship unsteady, even fiery. If the Rooster can control his or her nagging and give the Tiger some freedom, and if the Tiger can accept the Rooster's finicky nature, there may be some hope of harmony.

❈ Dog: 10

The Tiger and the Dog have potential for great mutual respect and loyalty. Both are laid back and informal, finding it easy to communicate with each other and perfectly complementing each other's approach to life. In addition, the Dog's clever nature helps them resolve any problems that arise.

❈ Pig: 8

The Pig and the Tiger have plenty of shared interests, making this a favourable combination. The Pig brings stability to the relationship, but would do well to take care not to become insecure over the Tiger's adventurous behaviour. Both these animals have considerable appetites, so beware of overindulgence!

❈ Rat: 6

The Tiger and the Rat both like to get their own way, which means that success in this relationship requires both individuals to learn to compromise when disagreements crop up. All in all, this pairing may in the end make a longer-lasting friendship than full-scale romantic relationship.

❈ Ox: 4

Attracted by their differences, at first these two seem to complement each other. However, before long the Ox and the Tiger will clash. The Tiger loves freedom and adventure, while the Ox wants security and quietude. Tuning in to each other's wavelengths in the long term could take enormous effort.

THE RABBIT IN RELATIONSHIPS

Kind; Affectionate; Sensitive; Moody; Restrained

Loving, considerate, nurturing and fun to be with, Rabbits are hard to resist! Rabbits look for security in their relationships, and can become needy if they don't find it. Any long-term romance has to have good financial prospects in order to accommodate the Rabbit's sophisticated tastes. When they do find "the one", Rabbits offer full commitment. Uncomfortable with conflict, Rabbits need to learn to address relationship issues as they arise, rather than suppressing them.

PATTERNS OF COMPATIBILITY AND CONFLICT

The Rabbit is most compatible with the Sheep and the Pig. These are all artistic, sensual and emotional people, who favour the quiet life. The Rooster is the Rabbit's diametrical opposite and the least compatible sign in the cycle.

RELATIONSHIPS AND COMPATIBILITY

The Rabbit in a relationship with the …

❋ RABBIT: 8

Two Rabbits obviously have much in common. They're capable of a healthy, loving relationship, with every chance of lasting harmony. However, this partnership could also be a bit on the safe and unadventurous side, and over-familiarity could have them upsetting each other's sensitivities.

❋ DRAGON: 6

Disparities in this combination may produce conflict, but there's potential for success. For the relationship to work, the Rabbit needs to accept the Dragon's dominant nature, and try not to be too sulky when things don't go his or her way. Both need to set shared objectives and pursue them together.

❋ SNAKE: 6

A relationship between a Snake and a Rabbit has the potential to be both passionate and relaxed. Both parties may need to make an effort to go out to find adventure together if the relationship is to survive in the long term, and overall there may simply be too little dynamism for success.

❋ HORSE: 4

Horses and Rabbits have very different views on life. The Horse may be too volatile, changeable and temperamental for the Rabbit; while the Rabbit's lack of interest in adventure may frustrate the Horse. Both parties would need to work hard at compromise in order to accommodate each other.

❋ SHEEP: 10

This is an ideal combination. Both Sheep and Rabbits love their homes and families, and both have sophisticated tastes. The only potential danger for their relationship is that it could become a little too comfortable. Open communication and getting out into the world are the keys to their happiness.

❋ MONKEY: 5

The Monkey can run rings around the Rabbit, and if the Monkey fails to show the Rabbit enough attention, the latter may develop trust issues. Rabbits may need reasons other than innate attraction to keep at this relationship – for example, if the Monkey shows support toward the Rabbit's objectives.

The Rabbit in Relationships

❈ **Rooster: 1**

The Rabbit's fixed Element of Wood is overridden by the Rooster's Metal, meaning that these two pretty much live on different planets with little hope of finding mutual ground. The Rooster's strong opinions and critical nature are anathema for the normally tolerant but also highly sensitive Rabbit.

❈ **Dog: 8**

Good levels of understanding and mutual trust make this a workable combination, both in love and business. Both people are kindly and gentle, and both have the possibility for great depth in their relationships. The Dog may bring out the more adventurous side of the often timorous Rabbit.

❈ **Pig: 10**

The Pig and the Rabbit have very similar outlooks on life. Sensitive souls, they display profound understanding of each other and can develop deep intimacy toward each other. These love birds are highly likely to want to nurture a happy home life, and to create a loving, supportive family unit.

❈ **Rat: 5**

This combination makes a wonderful friendship, but the Rabbit and the Rat may be too different to become promising lovers. They both appreciate security, but the unpredictable and nonstop nature of the Rat may prove too unsettling for the cautious, peace-loving Rabbit.

❈ **Ox: 7**

The Ox and the Rabbit both have qualities that complement each other to create a workable and contented romantic relationship. It may, however, appear a little dull (and makes for an undynamic business relationship), as neither wants to upset the status quo, take risks or go after life's thrills.

❈ **Tiger: 6**

A Rabbit with a Tiger shows potential for a workable combination, as long as each accepts the other's different communication style. The Rabbit's intuitive approach to life can help solve problems in the relationship, but the Tiger can make a meal of the Rabbit if the Rabbit doesn't know where he or she stands.

| RELATIONSHIPS AND COMPATIBILITY

THE DRAGON IN RELATIONSHIPS

Charismatic; Dominant; Attractive; Unpredictable; Dynamic

Enthusiastic, charming, and secure in themselves, Dragons find it easy to attract the attention of potential partners – in fact, they crave having people fall under their charismatic spell. When a Dragon falls in love, he or she tends to be open and honest – although not always easy to be with. Dragons may be intolerant of each other's weaknesses and can show a fierce temper. They're best suited to partners who will not be overwhelmed or brow-beaten by their dominant nature.

COMPATIBILITY AND CONFLICT

The Dragon is most compatible with the Monkey and the Rat. Highly creative, all three want to initiate projects and show high levels of ambition. The Dog is the Dragon's diametrical opposite and the least compatible sign in the cycle.

THE DRAGON IN RELATIONSHIPS 龍

The Dragon in a relationship with the …

✸ **Dragon: 7**

Two Dragons make a dynamic, confident and unified partnership that has potential to make great impact on the world. However, they do need to take care that their relationship doesn't become too competitive. This would be a good partnership for impassioned campaigning.

✸ **Snake: 8**

A Snake and a Dragon makes a good, respectful combination of signs. The Snake offers a restraining influence the Dragon's self-indulgent and often over-zealous self-belief. As long as these two respect each other's differences, this match has great potential for lasting happiness.

✸ **Horse: 7**

Dynamic, enthusiastic and sociable, this partnership has a strong sexual content, making it a viable proposition for success. However, these two also have the potential for competitiveness. Communication is key to making the pairing work. Both partners should take care not to neglect life's niggly detail.

✸ **Sheep: 7**

Mutual attraction may not be enough to keep this partnership alive. In order to achieve lasting harmony, the Sheep must accept the Dragon's free spirit and the Dragon must tone down his or her pushy nature. If they're able to do both these things, this relationship shows relatively good potential for success.

✸ **Monkey: 10**

These two proactive, dynamic signs create a lively partnership that shows great potential for long-term happiness. Mutually enchanted with one another, the Monkey and the Dragon are both able to stand up for themselves, and neither is ever fazed by the other's lively and exciting nature.

✸ **Rooster: 6**

This formidable combination can take on the world – and will probably win – but not without some serious clashes of ego on the way. The Rooster may bring the Dragon down to Earth, reining in his or her self-confidence. The relationship has the potential to work if both parties learn to compromise.

RELATIONSHIPS AND COMPATIBILITY

❂ **Dog: 1**

The Dragon and the Dog approach issues from very different perspectives, and neither is thoughtful enough to accommodate the other. Able to resist the Dragon's magnetism, the Dog is prepared to be critical of the Dragon when necessary – but at his or her peril, for nothing can anger the Dragon more.

❂ **Pig: 7**

A Pig and a Dragon will commit happily to a relationship, showing mutual understanding. The Pig won't mind that the Dragon is always the centre of attention, but the warlike Dragon should take care not to bully or try to overcome the peaceable Pig – who, if pushed too far, won't stand for it.

❂ **Rat: 10**

A fantastic combination! The Rat and the Dragon show great mutual understanding, without threatening each other. There's plenty of excitement and passion, but each also allows the other some space. With the Dragon's drive and the Rat's opportunism, this pairing can achieve great things.

❂ **Ox: 8**

This strong relationship is built on mutual attraction and admiration. Both the Ox and the Dragon are prepared to commit to each other and will work hard at achieving lasting harmony – despite their naturally unyielding natures. The Dragon will need to take account of the Ox's conservatism.

❂ **Tiger: 8**

A dynamic and dramatic combination of personalities, the Dragon and the Tiger make a strong team with a deep attraction that's all claws, excitement and passion. However, both parties may want to be in charge, so for long-term harmony they'll need to work out who will be the one to compromise.

❂ **Rabbit: 6**

Disparities in this combination may produce conflict, but there's potential for success. For the relationship to work, the Rabbit needs to accept the Dragon's dominant nature, and try not to be too sulky when things don't go his or her way. Both need to set shared objectives and pursue them together.

THE SNAKE IN RELATIONSHIPS

Beguiling; Sensual; Romantic; Charming; Loving

Alluring and passionate, the Snake is skilled in the art of seduction. He or she makes an intriguing partner – an enigma prone to secrecy, who will take a long time to reveal his or her true self. Snakes are home-loving individuals who enjoy quiet and comfort and will work hard to sustain a relationship with the right person. They can be choosy, though, and even once in a relationship may still like to flirt outside it – and yet become jealous if their partner does the same.

PATTERNS OF COMPATIBILITY AND CONFLICT

The Snake is most compatible with the Ox and the Rooster. All three of these animal signs represent dedication, determination and thoughtfulness. The Pig is the Snake's diametrical opposite and the least compatible in the cycle of signs.

RELATIONSHIPS AND COMPATIBILITY

The Snake in a relationship with the ...

- **Snake: 7**

    A favourable and co-operative partnership, two Snakes not only understand each other, but fully support and accommodate each other, too. With so little conflict, they may become over-familiar, so some independence from each other, such as pursuing different hobbies, may help keep the relationship alive.

- **Horse: 4**

    With their wildly different natures, and lack of empathy and understanding for each other, the Horse and the Snake make a troubled partnership that has little chance of longevity. To improve the prospects for success, both will have to work very hard at keeping open the channels of communication.

- **Sheep: 6**

    Attraction, sexual chemistry and possibly love could make this a workable combination of signs, but the lack of dynamism, adventurousness and discipline in both the Sheep and the Snake may hold back the relationship, and the individuals in it, from reaching their full potential.

- **Monkey: 4**

    There needs to be a good reason for these two to be together. Suspicious of each other, both the Monkey and the Snake find it difficult to empathize and each may even feel threatened by the other. With fundamentally different paces of life, too, there needs to be compromise on both sides.

- **Rooster: 10**

    The Rooster and the Snake are both realists, who are keen on security and have similar values in life. They communicate well and pursue the same interests, including making a home. All this, together with their deep trust of each other, means that this partnership shows excellent long-term prospects.

- **Dog: 8**

    This is a promising combination, characterized by attraction, respect and mental compatibility. The Snake will inevitably run the show, but the Dog is likely to be fine with that, happy to concede to the Snake's whims and tolerating his or her tendency to secrecy, jealousy or introversion.

THE SNAKE IN RELATIONSHIPS 蛇

✼ Pig: 1

Despite any initial attraction, the Snake's fixed Element of Fire and the Pig's Water make this a challenging combination, often dominated by the Snake. Totally different world-views mean that these two have very little in common: communication is difficult and each tends to be preoccupied by self-interest.

✼ Rat: 7

There's scope here for a successful romance, as long as both the Snake and the Rat acknowledge and respect each other's differences and try to develop mutual understanding. In the long term, both will need to deal with issues as soon as they arise and make sure they work at keeping their relationship alive.

✼ Ox: 10

The Ox and the Snake share their world-view. They're both caring and home-loving, putting their family above all. Neither looks for a wild or thrilling social life, instead being content to enjoy simple pleasures together. The Snake needs to be careful not to take advantage of the more naïve Ox.

✼ Tiger: 3

The Tiger may well be drawn to the Snake, but their different approaches to life and lack of natural empathy make it difficult for these two to trust each other. In addition, neither is likely to be able to persuade the other to his or her point of view, further reducing their chances for long-term harmony.

✼ Rabbit: 6

A relationship between a Snake and a Rabbit has the potential to be both passionate and relaxed. Both parties will need to make an effort to go out to find adventure together if the relationship is to stay the course, and overall there may simply be too little dynamism for success.

✼ Dragon: 8

A Snake and a Dragon makes a good, respectful combination of signs. The Snake offers a restraining influence for the Dragon's self-indulgent and often over-zealous self-belief. As long as these two respect each other's differences, this match has great potential for lasting happiness.

馬 | RELATIONSHIPS AND COMPATIBILITY

THE HORSE IN RELATIONSHIPS

Dynamic; Hasty; Restless; Spontaneous; Irresponsible

The Horse is the ultimate free spirit. Horses fall in love – or become infatuated – in an instant, claiming "This time it's the real thing!" However, they're ultimately flirtatious and fickle, at least until they find someone exciting enough to hold their interest. When they do, they can show passionate commitment. Potential partners need to allow Horses their freedom, resisting any urge to be possessive, and being happy to spend time alone, or to be constantly on the go.

PATTERNS OF COMPATIBILITY AND CONFLICT

The Horse is most compatible with the Tiger and the Dog. These signs have strong communication skills and are straightforward and outgoing. The Rat is the Horse's diametrical opposite and the least compatible sign in the cycle.

THE HORSE IN RELATIONSHIPS | 馬

The Horse in a relationship with the …

✤ **Horse: 6**

This dynamic partnership provides good foundations for a successful relationship, as long as both Horses share life goals and try not to compete for the limelight. They understand each other's need for spontaneity, and will be happy to give each other the freedom needed to expend their tireless energy.

✤ **Sheep: 9**

A strong attraction between these two signs means that the Sheep and the Horse make a great combination. The Horse leads the way in their life together, with the Sheep relishing the opportunity to step out of the rut to take part in some of the excitement on which the Horse thrives.

✤ **Monkey: 4**

Two competitive attention-seekers in the same relationship can make for a tricky ride! The Horse hates the feeling of being tied down by the Monkey, who can be made anxious by the Horse's need for freedom. This relationship works only if both feel that it's worth the effort of trying to find a connection.

✤ **Rooster: 6**

These two adventurers are instantly attracted to each other, although the Rooster plans the excitement, while the Horse simply finds it. In romance, these two may enter into a power struggle. The Horse may need to let the Rooster lead occasionally; the Rooster must learn to listen as well as to crow.

✤ **Dog: 10**

The Dog and the Horse have much in common – for example, both are outgoing and positive and both have a desire to explore the world. Best of all, the Dog is secure enough to accept the Horse's need for freedom, giving this pairing altogether excellent prospects for lasting happiness.

✤ **Pig: 5**

Sexual attraction may not be enough to keep this relationship alive in the long term. The Horse is far too capricious for the restrained Pig, while the Pig is too unadventurous for the Horse. The relationship can survive only if the Pig gives the Horse some freedom, and the Horse is careful not to neglect the Pig.

RELATIONSHIPS AND COMPATIBILITY

❀ **Rat: 1**

On the face of it, the Horse and the Rat appear to have much in common. At first, there may be mutual infatuation, but in fact these two want very different things from life and the relationship may be characterized by conflict. It could take considerable hard work for this partnership to stand the test of time.

❀ **Ox: 4**

Only mildly compatible, the Ox and the Horse do not show great prospects for a successful long-term relationship. The Horse is independent, restless and driven, while the Ox is slow, intellectual and reflective. The relationship can work only if there is sustained flexibility and tolerance from both partners.

❀ **Tiger: 10**

What adventures the Horse and the Tiger can have! Both take a positive approach to life, and share their need for excitement and new experiences. A relationship between these two is likely to be characterized by loyalty and respect – and that goes for professional relationships between them, too.

❀ **Rabbit: 4**

Horses and Rabbits have very different views on life. The Horse may be too volatile, changeable and temperamental for the Rabbit; while the Rabbit's lack of interest in adventure may frustrate the Horse. Both parties would need to work hard at compromise in order to accommodate each other.

❀ **Dragon: 7**

Dynamic, enthusiastic and sociable, this partnership has a strong sexual content, making it a viable proposition for success. However, these two also have the potential for competitiveness. Communication is key to making the pairing work. Both partners should take care not to neglect life's niggly detail.

❀ **Snake: 4**

With their wildly different natures, and lack of empathy and understanding for each other, the Horse and the Snake make an unhappy partnership that has little chance of longevity. To improve the prospects for success, both will have to work very hard at keeping open the channels of communication.

THE SHEEP IN RELATIONSHIPS

Gentle; Shy; Romantic; Sensual; Insecure

The gentle, sensuous Sheep needs an affectionate and intimate relationship that provides stability and protection. Only with a partner who is kind and caring can the creativity that lies within the Sheep begin to flourish. As Sheep tend not to be terribly outgoing, and will do anything to avoid causing themselves anxiety, it can take a while for them to find their perfect match. However, when they do they're fully committed to making a secure and loving home together for ever.

PATTERNS OF COMPATIBILITY AND CONFLICT

The Sheep is most compatible with the Rabbit and the Pig. These animals are all artistic, creative, sensual and refined, and they all favour a quiet life. The Ox is the Sheep's diametrical opposite and the least compatible on the cycle of signs.

羊 RELATIONSHIPS AND COMPATIBILITY

The Sheep in a relationship with the ...

❋ Sheep: 8

A quiet combination, simply seeking a happy life, two Sheep express deep empathy for one another and enjoy each other's capacity for sensuality. Neither is likely to take responsibility for the practicalities of life, and both may need to conjure up some drive and determination to get anything done.

❋ Monkey: 6

The Monkey's unpredictability and self-centredness can become too much for the insecure Sheep, and both may need to develop patience to make this relationship work. In addition, if the Monkey becomes too much of a bully, he or she may spark off the Sheep's more aggressive, ram-like tendencies.

❋ Rooster: 5

The sensitive Sheep may not cope well with the Rooster's outspoken nature; and the Rooster will be quick to criticize what he or she sees as the Sheep's wishy-washy nature. Nor will the Sheep appreciate being bossed around. Both need to make serious allowances for the other in order for this to work.

❋ Dog: 3

These two have little in common: they take life at a different pace, and have different aims. Dreamy and indecisive, the Sheep makes the proactive Dog impatient and frustrated, ultimately causing conflict. This pairing stands a chance of success only if the Sheep can be willing to follow the Dog's lead.

❋ Pig: 10

The Pig and the Sheep understand each other perfectly. They share emotional responses and are both sensual, peaceful, loving and caring. They're also both adaptable, and able to give each other space. Their refined tastes complement each other to create a harmonious environment for a happy life.

❋ Rat: 3

This challenging combination presents two very different attitudes to life and styles of self-expression. To make the partnership work, the Sheep needs to be more focused and organized, and the Rat more tolerant and appreciative. Each needs to develop a more caring attitude toward the other's feelings.

THE SHEEP IN RELATIONSHIPS 羊

❀ Ox: 1

There's simply no connection between the Ox and the Sheep – romantically or mentally. As neither of these people is terribly outspoken, there's likely to be conflict and unexpressed resentment, and very little excitement. The Ox may find the Sheep frivolous, and the Sheep may think the Ox uncivilized.

❀ Tiger: 5

The Sheep may provide a stabilizing influence on the Tiger, and the Tiger can look after the Sheep, but ultimately the Tiger will get bored with having to tread so carefully. Although the relationship may work as a business partnership, for lasting romance the Tiger needs more adventure.

❀ Rabbit: 10

This is an ideal combination. Sheep and Rabbits both love their homes and families, and both have sophisticated tastes. The only potential danger for their relationship is that it could become a little too comfortable. Open communication and getting out into the world are the keys to their happiness.

❀ Dragon: 7

Mutual attraction may not be enough to keep this partnership alive. In order to achieve lasting harmony, the Sheep is well advised to accept the Dragon's free spirit and the Dragon must tone down his or her pushy nature. If they're able to do these things, this relationship shows good potential for success.

❀ Snake: 6

Attraction, sexual chemistry and possibly love could make this a workable combination of signs, but the lack of dynamism, adventurousness and discipline in both the Sheep and the Snake may hold back the relationship, and the individuals in it, from reaching their full potential.

❀ Horse: 9

A strong attraction between these two signs means that the Sheep and the Horse make a great combination. The Horse leads the way in their life together, with the Sheep relishing the opportunity to step out of the rut and take part in some of the excitement on which the Horse thrives.

THE MONKEY IN RELATIONSHIPS

Provocative; Devious; Confident; Bossy; Proactive

Charming and amusing, Monkey people captivate and intrigue their potential partners. They thrive on excitement and unpredictability, which makes them stimulating people to hang out with; they never allow things to get dull. Their mischievous and fickle natures mean that early on they may flit from one person to another, but ultimately they make loyal partners who don't give up on anyone. The Monkey's ideal partner is flexible, stimulating and not over-sensitive.

PATTERNS OF COMPATIBILITY AND CONFLICT

The Monkey is most compatible with the Rat and the Dragon. Creative and active, these three initiate projects and press toward their goals. The Tiger is the Monkey's diametrical opposite and the least compatible sign in the cycle.

THE MONKEY IN RELATIONSHIPS 猴

The Monkey in a relationship with the …

✺ **Monkey: 8**

Two Monkeys have so much positivity bouncing between them that their relationship is well placed to achieve greatness. United in their attitudes to life and heading for mutually beneficial goals, these two need only to take care that neither tries to outdo the other, as they'll both want to be in charge.

✺ **Rooster: 5**

The Monkey's humour can lighten up the serious Rooster, but the Rooster's pickiness and critical nature may in the end prove too much for the fun-loving Monkey. For this relationship to work, both are well advised to develop high levels of tolerance and learn to give the other a great deal of leeway.

✺ **Dog: 6**

As long as the tricky Monkey remembers not to rush off and leave the Dog in the dark about its schemes, and the Dog is prepared to remain committed to the relationship, there is some hope here. Indeed, the Dog's character is well-suited to appreciating the Monkey's opportunistic nature.

✺ **Pig: 8**

Sociable and interested in other people, these signs are instantly attracted to one another. However, to help the relationship last, the Monkey should accommodate the Pig's preference for staying at home; and the Pig might learn to communicate more openly and explore the outside world a little, too.

✺ **Rat: 10**

The Monkey and the Rat have similar outlooks on life and display plenty of mutual respect and understanding. There's also mutual attraction and a shared need for excitement. As long as they remember to talk things through when they need to, this relationship has every possibility for lasting happiness.

✺ **Ox: 6**

Although it's likely to work better in business than in love, this is a reasonably compatible combination. The Ox and the Monkey may find it difficult to understand each other's way of life, and may have to work hard to appreciate their differences, but if they're able to build trust, there's potential for fun.

RELATIONSHIPS AND COMPATIBILITY

❀ Tiger: 1

The Tiger's fixed Element of Wood conflicts with the Monkey's Metal, so although opposites may initially attract, in the long term it's unlikely that these two will understand one another. They're also both highly competitive. It would take a great deal of compromise for the relationship to work.

❀ Rabbit: 5

The Monkey can run rings around the Rabbit, and if the Monkey fails to show the Rabbit enough attention, the latter may develop trust issues. Rabbits need reasons other than innate attraction to keep at this relationship – for example, if the Monkey shows support toward the Rabbit's objectives.

❀ Dragon: 10

These two proactive, dynamic signs create a lively partnership that shows great potential for lasting happiness. Mutually enchanted with each other, the Monkey and the Dragon are both able to stand up for themselves, and neither is ever fazed by the other's lively and exciting nature.

❀ Snake: 4

There needs to be a good reason for these two to be together. Suspicious of one another, both the Monkey and the Snake find it difficult to empathize and each may even feel threatened by the other. With fundamentally different paces of life, too, there needs to be compromise on both sides.

❀ Horse: 4

Two competitive attention-seekers in the same relationship makes for a tricky ride! The Horse hates the feeling of being tied down by the Monkey, who can be made anxious by the Horse's need for freedom. This relationship can work only if both feel that it's worth the effort of trying to find a connection.

❀ Sheep: 6

The Monkey's unpredictability and self-centredness can become too much for the insecure Sheep, and both will need to develop patience to make this relationship work. In addition, if the Monkey becomes too much of a bully, he or she may spark off the Sheep's more aggressive, ram-like tendencies.

RELATIONSHIPS AND COMPATIBILITY

THE ROOSTER IN RELATIONSHIPS
Pompous; Critical; Good-hearted; Bossy; Sensitive

The charming, well-presented and elegant Rooster knows how to make a good first impression, but is not an easy sign to get along with in an intimate partnership – thin-skinned individuals who cannot take frequent and unsolicited feedback simply need not apply. However, underneath all that, Roosters are good-hearted characters, who make steady and faithful lovers, and are surprisingly sensitive to being criticized themselves.

PATTERNS OF COMPATIBILITY AND CONFLICT
The Rooster is most compatible with the Ox and the Snake. All three of these animals take a dedicated, determined and thoughtful approach to life. The Rabbit is the Rooster's diametrical opposite and the least compatible sign in the cycle.

RELATIONSHIPS AND COMPATIBILITY

The Rooster in a relationship with the …

❀ ROOSTER: 2

Two Roosters are far too competitive to make for a harmonious relationship. The constant struggles to rule the roost create endless conflict and neither Rooster can bear to be micro-managed or to take criticism from the other. The only hope for success is for both to develop some diplomacy and tact.

❀ DOG: 6

In this challenging combination, the Rooster is concerned with formalities, hard work and showing off, while the Dog wants flexible working and to relax completely when the job is done. Furthermore, the Rooster will need to go out of his or her way to demonstrate a more caring side to the Dog.

❀ PIG: 8

The thick-skinned Pig is one person who is able to put up with the Rooster's lack of tact. Able to see beneath the brash, logical exterior, the Pig offers the Rooster security and emotional intelligence. In return, the Rooster needs to make sure that he or she develops the ability to communicate more sensitively.

❀ RAT: 4

Their competitive natures mean that the Rat and the Rooster present a conflicting combination. With time and effort from both, each might come to appreciate the other's qualities and ability to make a positive contribution to the relationship, but probably more successfully in business than in romance.

❀ OX: 10

A harmonious combination that shows love, passion and respect on both sides, the Ox and the Rooster share similar values – both dedicate themselves to getting a job done and both believe in the importance of authority and orderliness. All in all, there is wonderful potential for lasting happiness.

❀ TIGER: 6

Two attention-seekers in the same relationship can lead to competition, making the relationship unsteady, even fiery. If the Rooster can control his or her nagging and give the Tiger some freedom, and if the Tiger can accept the Rooster's finicky nature, there may be some hope of harmony.

The Rooster in Relationships

- **Rabbit: 1**

  The Rabbit's fixed Element of Wood is overridden by the Rooster's Metal, meaning that these two pretty much live on different planets, with little hope of finding mutual ground. The Rooster's strong opinions and critical nature can be anathema to the normally tolerant but also highly sensitive Rabbit.

- **Dragon: 6**

  This formidable combination can take on the world – and will probably win – but not without some serious clashes of ego on the way. The Rooster will bring the Dragon down to Earth, reining in his or her self-confidence. The relationship has the potential to work if both parties learn to compromise.

- **Snake: 10**

  The Rooster and the Snake are both realists, who are keen on security and have similar values in life. They communicate well and pursue the same interests, including making a home. All this, together with their deep trust of each other, means that this partnership shows excellent long-term prospects.

- **Horse: 6**

  These two adventurers are instantly attracted to each other, although the Rooster plans the excitement, while the Horse simply finds it. In romance, these two may enter into a power struggle. The Horse may need to let the Rooster lead occasionally; the Rooster must learn to listen as well as to crow.

- **Sheep: 5**

  The sensitive Sheep may not cope well with the Rooster's outspoken nature; and the Rooster will be quick to criticize what he or she sees as the Sheep's wishy-washy nature. Nor will the Sheep appreciate being bossed around. Both need to make serious allowances for the other in order for this work.

- **Monkey: 5**

  The Monkey's humour can lighten up the serious Rooster, but the Rooster's pickiness and critical nature may in the end prove too much for the fun-loving Monkey. For this relationship to work, both would be well advised to develop high levels of tolerance and to learn to give the other a great deal of leeway.

THE DOG IN RELATIONSHIPS

Honest; Protective; Loyal; Suspicious; Worrisome

It takes time for the Dog person to get to know and trust someone enough to give away his or her heart. However, once in a relationship, Dogs are fiercely loyal and expect loyalty, companionship and affection in return. These are honest individuals who can be badly hurt by any kind of deception, and they hate to be left alone. Prone to worry, a Dog is well advised to find a partner who is confident and who can encourage the Dog out of his or her shell.

PATTERNS OF COMPATIBILITY AND CONFLICT

The Dog is most compatible with the Tiger and the Horse. Straightforward and outgoing, these signs are able to communicate well with other people. The Dragon is the Dog's diametrical opposite and the least compatible sign in the cycle.

THE DOG IN RELATIONSHIPS 狗

The Dog in a relationship with the …

✸ **Dog: 8**

Once their relationship is established, two Dogs show a naturally good understanding of each other and are able to put each other at ease. They're caring and affectionate together, but also have the motivation and courage to deal with any challenges that threaten their security.

✸ **Pig: 7**

A Dog and a Pig have reasonable potential for harmony. Both have considerable emotional warmth and a love of family. The Pig reassures the worrier in the Dog, while the Dog is likely to come to the Pig's rescue whenever necessary. The Dog also helps temper the Pig's tendency to excess.

✸ **Rat: 7**

Despite their different interests, the Rat and the Dog appreciate that they each bring something beneficial to a relationship, giving this one good potential for lasting harmony. There are unlikely to be fireworks and passion, but a good, stable bond that with good communication can stand the test of time.

✸ **Ox: 5**

The Ox and the Dog show little attraction or empathy, and have little in common – they're simply ill at ease with each other. To make the relationship work romantically, both parties would need to share similar life goals, but as a campaigning partnership, there's potential for success.

✸ **Tiger: 10**

The Tiger and the Dog have potential for great mutual respect and loyalty. Both are laid back and informal, finding it easy to communicate with one another and perfectly complementing each other's approach to life. In addition, the Dog's clever nature helps them resolve any problems that arise.

✸ **Rabbit: 8**

Good levels of understanding and mutual trust make this a workable combination, in both love and business. Both signs are kindly and gentle, and both have the possibility for great depth in their relationships. The Dog may bring out the more adventurous side of the often timorous Rabbit.

RELATIONSHIPS AND COMPATIBILITY

❈ **Dragon: 1**

The Dragon and the Dog approach issues from very different perspectives, and neither is considerate enough to make any compromise. Able to resist the Dragon's magnetism, the Dog is prepared to be critical of the Dragon when necessary – but at his or her peril, for nothing will anger the Dragon more.

❈ **Snake: 8**

This is a promising combination, characterized by attraction, respect and mental compatibility. The Snake will inevitably run the show, but the Dog is likely to be fine with that, happy to concede to the Snake's whims and tolerating his or her tendency to secrecy, jealousy or introversion.

❈ **Horse: 10**

The Dog and the Horse have much in common – for example, both are outgoing and positive and both have a desire to explore the world. Best of all, the Dog is secure enough to accept the Horse's need for freedom, giving this pairing altogether excellent prospects for lasting happiness.

❈ **Sheep: 3**

These two have little in common: they take life at a different pace, and have different aims. Dreamy and indecisive, the Sheep can make the proactive Dog impatient and frustrated, ultimately causing conflict. This pairing stands a chance of success only if the Sheep is willing to follow the Dog's lead.

❈ **Monkey: 6**

As long as the tricky Monkey remembers not to rush off and leave the Dog in the dark about its schemes, and the Dog is prepared to remain committed to the relationship, there is some hope here. Indeed, the Dog is well poised to appreciate the Monkey's opportunistic nature.

❈ **Rooster: 6**

In this challenging combination, the Rooster is concerned with formalities, hard work and showing off, while the Dog wants flexible working and to relax completely when the job is done. Furthermore, the Rooster will need to go out of his or her way to demonstrate to the Dog a more caring side.

THE PIG IN RELATIONSHIPS

Dedicated; Kind-hearted; Pleasure-loving; Gullible; Passionate

Pigs are at their best in a secure, settled relationship with a loving partner to whom they can be totally committed. Sensual and sexual, Pigs may be particularly raunchy when they're young, but grow up to become gentle home-makers who don't like to cause trouble for anyone. They should take care not to be too naïve when choosing a partner, remembering that unscrupulous people may take advantage of their kind natures; and they should avoid someone who is bossy.

PATTERNS OF COMPATIBILITY AND CONFLICT

The Pig is most compatible with the Rabbit and the Sheep. Artistic, sensual and emotional, all these animals want to lead a quiet, refined life. The Snake is the Pig's diametrical opposite and the least compatible sign in the cycle.

RELATIONSHIPS AND COMPATIBILITY

The Pig in a relationship with the …

✸ Pig: 5

Despite initial lust, two pigs are too alike for lasting harmony. They tend to bring out the worst in each other – both are likely to become stubborn, live a sedentary life of excess, and become reclusive and unadventurous. In addition, they'll need to work hard to keep communication channels open.

✸ Rat: 7

There's plenty of excitement and attraction in this promising combination, which has good potential for a loving relationship that works as a result of companionship as well as romance. In order for the bond to stand the test of time, the Rat will need to acknowledge and respect the Pig's need for stability.

✸ Ox: 8

The Pig has the potential to bring out in the Ox a sense of adventure, which is just what he or she needs. Coupled with mutual attraction and potential for deep friendship, this relationship shows great promise. Both may need to be prepared to keep working through any differences as they arise.

✸ Tiger: 8

The Pig and the Tiger have plenty of shared interests, making this a favourable combination. The Pig brings stability to the relationship, but may need to take care not to become insecure over the Tiger's adventurous behaviour. Both these animals have considerable appetites, so beware overindulgence!

✸ Rabbit: 10

The Pig and the Rabbit have very similar outlooks on life. Sensitive souls, they display profound mutual understanding and can develop deep intimacy toward each other. These love birds are highly likely to want to nurture a happy home life, and to create a loving, supportive family unit.

✸ Dragon: 7

A Pig and a Dragon will happily commit to a relationship, showing mutual understanding. The Pig won't mind that the Dragon is always the centre of attention, but the warlike Dragon should take care not to bully or try to overcome the peaceable Pig – who, if pushed too far, won't stand for it.

THE PIG IN RELATIONSHIPS 豬

❈ Snake: 1

Despite any initial attraction, the Snake's fixed Element of Fire and the Pig's Water make this a challenging combination, often dominated by the Snake. Totally different world-views mean that these two have very little in common: communication is difficult and each tends to be preoccupied by self-interest.

❈ Horse: 5

Sexual attraction may not be enough to keep this relationship alive in the long term. The Horse is far too capricious for the restrained Pig, while the Pig is too unadventurous for the Horse. The relationship can survive only if the Pig gives the Horse some freedom, and the Horse is careful not to neglect the Pig.

❈ Sheep: 10

The Pig and the Sheep understand each other perfectly. They share emotional responses and both are sensual, peaceful, loving and caring. They're also both adaptable, and able to give each other space. Their refined tastes complement each other to create a harmonious environment for a happy life.

❈ Monkey: 8

Sociable and interested in other people, these signs are instantly attracted to each other. However, to help the relationship last, the Monkey should accommodate the Pig's preference for staying at home; and the Pig might learn to communicate more openly and explore the outside world a little, too.

❈ Rooster: 8

The thick-skinned Pig is one person who is able to put up with the Rooster's lack of tact. Able to see beneath the brash, logical exterior, the Pig offers the Rooster security and emotional intelligence. In return, the Rooster needs to make sure that he or she develops the ability to communicate more sensitively.

❈ Dog: 7

A Dog and a Pig have reasonable potential for harmony. Both have considerable emotional warmth and a love of family. The Pig reassures the worrier in the Dog, while the Dog is likely to come to the Pig's rescue whenever necessary. The Dog also helps temper the Pig's tendency to excess.

CHAPTER THREE

PROSPECTS OVER TIME

In this chapter we examine the year of influence of each animal sign to reveal in what ways the animals exert their energy on the fortunes of the world at large and on the animals found in each individual horoscope. Sometimes a sign's energies will modify our prospects in favourable ways – for example, improving potential for success or relationships. Sometimes the influence will be less favourable, in which case certain animal types will need to control or temporarily amend their behaviour in order to overcome challenges or obstacles. However, it's important to remember that Chinese astrology doesn't interpret prospects simplistically in terms of "good" and "bad". So, even when a particular year presents challenging influences, these more tricky times can give us the opportunity to develop in ways that make us altogether stronger. Indeed, each person's total fortunes over the whole 12-year cycle are regarded as a complete, appropriate and valuable experience – even when they don't uphold the more Western, fairytale wish for life to be easy and wonderful all the time.

鼠	牛	虎
兔	龍	蛇
馬	羊	猴
雞	狗	豬

PROSPECTS OVER TIME

YEAR INFLUENCES AND YOUR BIRTH SIGNS

The animal sign governing a particular year predisposes us to likely benefits, challenges, and matters to take special care over. It also suggests strategies that each of us can adopt in order to produce the best possible results in that year.

When you look for advice in this chapter, you need to interpret two types of influence to help you plan life decisions, bearing in mind that your prospects follow a 12-year cycle. So, for example, there will be several years in your cycle that show more auspicious prospects for your home life. If you're planning to start a family, choose a year that's favourable for family and/or home to start trying for a baby. The two determinants of your prospects in any year are:

1 the general characteristics associated with the prevailing animal sign of the year (for example, loyalty in the year of the Dog; adventure in the year of the Horse; and so on), which apply to people collectively;
2 how the signs from your year and month of birth interact with the prevailing year sign (the patterns of interaction are closely related to how the signs work together in relationships; see Chapter Two).

These two areas of influence can be considered in tandem. The effect arising from the interaction of your particular animal sign with that of the year will be the predominant influence on you as an individual, while the generic year influence will tend to affect you contextually. For example, the year of the Dragon (such as 2012 or 2024) is traditionally regarded as an influence toward more dramatic economic movements. Individuals will be affected by these collective influences, but will experience quite different personal prospects. The way in which a birth sign relates to a year sign falls into one of five categories:

YEAR INFLUENCES AND YOUR BIRTH SIGNS

1 The two signs are partners in a Triangle of Affinity (see p.154) – this presents the most favourable combination.
2 The birth sign is the same as the year sign – this presents a generally favourable combination.
3 The two signs are complementary paired signs in the cycle of signs (see each sign's analysis in Chapter One) – this gives a generally favourable combination;
4 The two signs sit opposite each other on the Circle of Conflict (see diagram, p.155) – this presents the least favourable combination.
5 The two signs fall into none of these categories, and therefore vary in their compatibility, case by case, but less extremely than categories 1 to 4.

MAKING THE MOST OF YOUR POTENTIAL EVERY YEAR

Traditional Chinese astrology is both pragmatic and holistic about how to make the best possible experience of life. Over the following pages, you'll see that certain guiding principles emerge from the analyses.

- Try to work with the prevailing energies and tendencies of the particular year, rather than fighting them or trying to change them according to your perceived preferences.
- Interpret the influences of each year as part of a more important overall pattern – be patient: remember, in challenging years, more favourable times lie ahead.
- Don't overstretch yourself – advice that's equally relevant to times when things are going well as it is to more challenging times.
- View challenging years, and those lacking dramatic outward progress, as periods when you can turn your energies inward, working on personal growth.
- When your own prospects for a certain action aren't favourable, be prepared to enlist the help of others who might be subject to more favourable influences.
- Look back over events of previous years and re-interpret them in the light of the information you now possess. In this way you can better understand your own experiences, and use this understanding to moderate your experience in future years.

鼠 PROSPECTS OVER TIME

THE YEAR OF THE RAT

RAT YEARS: 2008 (EARTH), 2020 (METAL), 2032 (WATER)
FIXED ELEMENT: WATER   YANG SIGN

KEYWORDS
• LIVELINESS • ACTION • CREATIVITY • INVENTION • INITIATION
• DEVELOPMENT • CONSTRUCTION • ANXIETY

GENERAL PROSPECTS

Like the typical characteristics of the Rat sign itself, years under the auspices of the Rat are packed with proactive experiences, lots of movement and lots of fresh, new ideas.

As the Rat represents the first year in the 12-year cycle of signs, Rat years are traditionally considered to be a time of new beginnings. Chinese astrologers believe that any new venture started in a Rat year is likely to face a positive future and will go on to exert its influence over years to come. If you have any plans for starting a new business, building a home or extension, or embarking upon a new relationship, doing so in the Year of the Rat can set you off on a positive footing. However, with so much energy in a state of flux during a Rat year, some people may find this time destabilizing and unsettling.

The year of the Rat for the …

🐾 RAT

In their own year, Rats can make the most of their innate qualities, riding high on the energy for change – and must only be careful not to take on too much.

🐾 OX

This is a favourable time for the Ox to make good progress in his or her ventures. Rat energy can help overcome Ox conservatism and "stuckness".

THE YEAR OF THE RAT 鼠

❊ **Tiger**

Extra energy from the Rat can tempt the Tiger into unwise action, so he or she is advised to avoid taking risks. This is a great year for making new contacts.

❊ **Rabbit**

Rabbits are generally unadventurous, so Rat years can give them the courage to strike out in a new direction and make exciting plans for the future.

❊ **Dragon**

Using cleverness rather than force, the Dragon may take up opportunities to achieve great things in romance, innovation and finance in a Rat year.

❊ **Snake**

Snakes become uncharacteristically lively in a Rat year, so they could take the opportunity to engage in new activities – and feel safer as they do so.

❊ **Horse**

The Horse finds a Rat year the most challenging. Rather than striking out, he or she might pursue self-development and save problem-solving for next year.

❊ **Sheep**

The Rat lends the Sheep more cleverness, dynamism and courage, making this a good year for active progress, professionally, intellectually and socially.

❊ **Monkey**

The Rat and the Monkey are kindred spirits, so this is a particularly favourable year for the Monkey to move forward with good ideas and new developments.

❊ **Rooster**

In this challenging year for finance, relationships and progress, Roosters should focus on dealing with outstanding matters rather than new plans.

❊ **Dog**

Rat influence brings Dog types out of themselves and enables them to be more daring and dynamic, and achieve success on a more adventurous scale.

❊ **Pig**

This is the best time for the home-loving Pig to try new experiences and fresh starts, although he or she may also expect to feel a little unsettled.

THE YEAR OF THE OX

OX YEARS: 2009 (EARTH), 2021 (METAL), 2033 (WATER)
FIXED ELEMENT: EARTH   YIN SIGN

KEYWORDS
• STABILITY • SECURITY • TOIL • PROGRESS • COMMITMENT •
• FRUSTRATION • SOLIDITY • CONSTRUCTION • PATIENCE •

GENERAL PROSPECTS

The Ox is a patient, steadfast and hardworking creature, and it's these qualities that benefit people collectively during an Ox year. Those who are prepared to commit themselves to a task and toil ceaselessly at bringing it to its conclusion can benefit in the year of the Ox, as can those who avoid excessive risk. People born under more energetic or erratic animal signs, such as the Dragon or the Monkey, may find that the year is better for them if they pursue more traditional or conservative ideals or objectives – perhaps working on enlarging or improving the home, for example, rather than trying to climb the world's highest peak or embarking upon some other daring adventure. Partnerships that begin in the year of the Ox are based on firm foundations, with logical and practical undertones. This is a favourable year for entering into business ventures with other people.

The year of the Ox for the …

Rat
As the Rat begins to see the benefits of last year's new ventures, he or she is advised to try not to race ahead, but nurture the effects like an Ox – patiently.

Ox
Oxen feel comfortable this year, building solid foundations for the years to come. They should try not to overdo the hard work, making time for fun, too.

THE YEAR OF THE OX 牛

❋ **Tiger**

Tigers are frustrated by slow progress in an Ox year, but can minimize their discontent by postponing any major decisions until next year.

❋ **Rabbit**

An Ox year is an auspicious time for the timid Rabbit to make decisions about his or her future, build relationships and perhaps even extend the family.

❋ **Dragon**

Steady Ox energy can encourage the Dragon to be more considered and less controversial in his or her objectives – for which the Dragon will reap rewards.

❋ **Snake**

Ox patterns suit the Snake, making this a good year for the Snake to follow his or her instincts, taking positive steps in business, finance and romance.

❋ **Horse**

The Horse's adventurous instincts are thwarted in an Ox year. If the Horse can hold fast in his or her present situation, the yields will be great next year.

❋ **Sheep**

This is a challenging, troublesome year for the Sheep, who is well advised to keep his or her head down, remain patient, and make few changes.

❋ **Monkey**

The Monkey's energetic instincts for world domination need reining in this year – it's better instead for him or her to focus on family and the home.

❋ **Rooster**

This is a great year for the Rooster, who has potential to make rapid progress and reap big rewards in work and love. He or she must seize every opportunity.

❋ **Dog**

The Dog should stick to domestic matters during an Ox year, as big plans and new ventures may prove unsatisfying at this time. Next year will be better.

❋ **Pig**

The Pig's instincts can be well tuned for an Ox year, allowing him or her to make quiet, confident progress in a context of stable, reliable energy.

PROSPECTS OVER TIME

THE YEAR OF THE TIGER

TIGER YEARS: 2010 (METAL), 2022 (WATER)
FIXED ELEMENT: WOOD   YANG SIGN

KEYWORDS
• VOLATILITY • HYPERACTIVITY • CONFIDENCE • DYNAMISM
• UNSTEADINESS • EXCITEMENT • PASSION • DRAMA • EXTRAVAGANCE

GENERAL PROSPECTS

During the year of the Tiger, all the signs of the Chinese horoscope may at times find themselves overwhelmed by strong emotions – even if extremes of feeling are normally completely out of character. Dramatic events as well as disturbances in the status quo are also likely. Even when there's no overall drama, life tends to move along apace in a Tiger year.

For some the speed of Tiger energy can cause turmoil; for others it can become a source of courage and adventure. In fact, during a Tiger year, even the most extravagant plans stand a chance of working out. On the world stage, a Tiger year may host advances in attempts to unite nations or organize world events – or it can have the opposite effect, causing political instability and even conflict, depending upon how the powers channel all that Tiger energy.

The year of the Tiger for the …

❋ RAT
  This year's dramatic potential may tempt the Rat into ever-more daring ventures, but Rats should beware big risks, which could result in big disasters.

❋ OX
  As the Ox hates drama, this may be a challenging year, littered with upsets and personal conflict. However, the Ox's steady head will see him or her through.

The Year of the Tiger 虎

- **Tiger**
 Tigers are finally free of the constraints of last year and in their element. They should not abandon all caution if they're to make the best of opportunities.
- **Rabbit**
 The Tiger's confident energies create an environment in which the usually timorous Rabbit is able to leap ahead with plans and grab opportunities.
- **Dragon**
 Volatile Tiger energy may afford Dragons exciting opportunities for self-advancement, but on the other hand may destabilize personal relationships.
- **Snake**
 Tiger energy can feel uncomfortable for the passive Snake, so this is a year for him or her to keep a low profile, avoiding any worldly adventure or risk.
- **Horse**
 This could be an active and expensive year for the Horse, who relishes the opportunities for business, personal advancement … and partying!
- **Sheep**
 Tiger energy can unsettle the steady Sheep, but Sheep are well advised to grab the chance for advancement, especially if they have allies who can help them.
- **Monkey**
 Tiger and Monkey energies clash, so this year Monkeys need to take care, stay calm and maintain the status quo – there are better years to achieve greatness.
- **Rooster**
 Roosters can cope brilliantly with the quick-fire demands of a year dominated by Tiger energy. With sharp focus, they can race toward their goals.
- **Dog**
 This is an auspicious year for Dogs, who are poised to be lucky in love and adventure. They can expect to have exciting ideas and glowing reputations.
- **Pig**
 Pigs are generally uncomfortable among Tiger energy, feeling there's too much instability. They might keep their biggest ambitions in check for another time.

兔 PROSPECTS OVER TIME

THE YEAR OF THE RABBIT

RABBIT YEARS: 2011 (METAL), 2023 (WATER)
FIXED ELEMENT: WOOD   YIN SIGN

KEYWORDS
• CALM • PEACE • STILLNESS • RELAXATION • REWARD
• SECURITY • HOME-MAKING • COMPASSION • DIPLOMACY

GENERAL PROSPECTS

Last year's Tiger energies caused daring excitement and, for some, high levels of uncertainty. This year, however, the energies of the Rabbit can make life feel much more peaceful. All the signs, even those prone to over-excitement, may find that this is a favourable year for resolving differences. Most will feel more compassion, compromise and understanding toward others, meaning that advancement may be founded on the well-being of others as well as the self. However, this level of harmony and gentle progress can be frustrating for some of the more impatient signs. On the world stage, there's a good deal of diplomacy in politics, with leaders coming together to foster collaboration between nations; conflicts may even come to peaceful conclusions. A Rabbit year can also be an auspicious time for the worlds of art and culture – this year, people can find their creative selves.

The year of the Rabbit for the …

❀ **RAT**

For the Rat, everything seems on hold in a Rabbit year, so Rats are best placed to deal with home matters, leaving business changes for more energetic times.

❀ **OX**

This year the Ox can make happy, steady progress, without feeling any need to rush. This is a good year for relationships, including romantic ones.

THE YEAR OF THE RABBIT 兔

✺ Tiger
The Rabbit and the Tiger have complementary qualities, so this year the Tiger need make no special effort in order to achieve progress and satisfaction.

✺ Rabbit
Rabbits can prosper in business, relationships, family matters and all-round well-being this year. Good opportunities are more likely to come their way.

✺ Dragon
Dragons should take things easy this year, collecting the rewards of last year's ventures and waiting for next year for another burst of activity.

✺ Snake
Snakes could try to be more straightforward, like the Rabbit, this year, and avoid the temptation toward deviousness, particularly in dealings with others.

✺ Horse
Frustrating as it may be, Horses are advised to focus their energies on home and family this year, avoiding change and saving new ventures for next year.

✺ Sheep
Sheep are very much at ease with Rabbit energies, giving excellent prospects for fun, and for success in finance, at work, and in partnerships of all kinds.

✺ Monkey
Monkeys can discover a spirit of entrepreneurship in a Rabbit year, initiating new ideas and projects, and preparing to watch them bloom next year.

✺ Rooster
Rooster and Rabbit energies conflict, so this is a time for the Rooster to rein things in, accept support and concentrate on putting their affairs in order.

✺ Dog
Taking opportunities, embarking on new relationships, starting new ventures and making acquisitions all stand a good chance of success for Dogs this year.

✺ Pig
Pig and Rabbit energies complement one another, making this a good year that provides excellent opportunities for personal and professional progress.

THE YEAR OF THE DRAGON

DRAGON YEARS: 2000 (METAL), 2012 (WATER), 2024 (WOOD)
FIXED ELEMENT: EARTH   YANG SIGN

KEYWORDS
• ADVENTURE • CREATIVITY • DARING • EXCITEMENT • PROMISE •
• INNOVATION • CHAOS • RECKLESSNESS • ABANDON • CRISIS MANAGEMENT •

GENERAL PROSPECTS

Dragon energies are adventurous, tempestuous and all-consuming, and with the prospect of these characteristics the year of the Dragon displays a dramatic shift from the relatively quiet interlude of the previous year of the Rabbit. In personal experiences, as well as on the world stage, there are bigger ventures, bigger successes (and also bigger failures) and generally more adventurous prevailing winds. The result is that the extrovert signs, such as the Rat and the Tiger, find the year of the Dragon exciting and full of promise; while more introverted, less daring signs, such as the Pig and the Rabbit, feel some discomfort and unease. In politics the year of the Dragon has potential for global economic shifts – positively and negatively. This is also a year for innovation and for those who need rescuing to find help through the Dragon's knack for crisis management.

The year of the Dragon for the …

RAT
The Rat and the Dragon are kindred spirits, so Dragon influence brings the Rat welcome drama, risk and activity. Rats can benefit in love and money.

OX
Oxen find Dragon years too volatile, with too much potential for disaster. They can use their innate sensibilities and caution to see them through.

THE YEAR OF THE DRAGON 龍

❈ **Tiger**

Sharing the Dragon's love of excitement and risk, Tigers grab the opportunity for dramatic forward progress, both materially and in relationships.

❈ **Rabbit**

Dragon years are tricky for the Rabbit, who needs to work at staying cheerful throughout. Rabbits should try not to become uncharacteristically impetuous.

❈ **Dragon**

Dragons are really in the groove in their own year. Excitement, successes, love, drama, thrills and spills – life is a roller coaster, and the Dragon loves it!

❈ **Snake**

Snakes hate unpredictability, but these are complementary signs so Snakes can deal with Dragon chaos, drawing on innate resilience until things calm down.

❈ **Horse**

Horses find that a Dragon year's spontaneity and opportunism enable them to build relationships, find romance and enjoy the altogether hectic ride.

❈ **Sheep**

Sheep need to conserve their resources for the challenges of a Dragon year. They may encounter positive developments, though, and emerge unscathed.

❈ **Monkey**

The Monkey is totally at home in the Dragon milieu, finding creativity and success. Monkeys are well advised to calm down by year's end, however.

❈ **Rooster**

In a Dragon year, the Rooster can run free, abandon caution and go for gold, with favourable chances for success and advancement.

❈ **Dog**

This is a tough year for the Dog, presenting obstacles and potential for worry. Dogs could lie low, conserve money, and rely on others whenever possible.

❈ **Pig**

Moderately beneficial for the Pig, a Dragon year is a good time for him or her to be more outgoing, socializing with others and getting noticed.

PROSPECTS OVER TIME

THE YEAR OF THE SNAKE

SNAKE YEARS: 2001 (METAL), 2013 (WATER), 2025 (WOOD)
FIXED ELEMENT: FIRE   YIN SIGN

KEYWORDS
• INTRIGUE • MYSTERY • SECRECY • SUBTERFUGE • INVENTIVENESS
• ROMANCE • RELATIONSHIP-BUILDING • CONSOLIDATION

GENERAL PROSPECTS

Things may not always be as they seem during the year of the Snake, with subterfuge and unrevealed insight potentially lurking like snakes themselves under every stone. On the world stage, this may mean that there are elaborate spy missions afoot, or it might simply mean lots of closed meetings behind the doors of power. At the human level, it can be easy to feel that others are keeping secrets or hiding things – less subtle animal types, such as the Monkey and the Horse, can find this level of secrecy (whether real or perceived) something of a challenge, as they don't know exactly how they stand. Similarly, skittish animal types, such as the Rat, may find that the idea that others are keeping things from them taps into their neuroses. For those who respond positively to Snake energies, this is a particularly good year for forming and consolidating relationships.

The year of the Snake for the …

- RAT

    Rats are uncomfortable with deception, so they should steel themselves for the unexpected and not take anything on trust. Flexibility is the key to coping.

- OX

    The Ox and the Snake are kindred spirits, so this year has excellent prospects. Expect rewards from previous efforts and seize chances in work and romance.

THE YEAR OF THE SNAKE 蛇

- **Tiger**
  Snake influences make it particularly hard for Tigers to connect with others. They're well advised to take close relationships slowly to remain unscathed.
- **Rabbit**
  Rabbit intuition is spot-on during a Snake year, so Rabbits can press forward and get good results professionally. Romance may not be as straightforward.
- **Dragon**
  Dragon efforts come to fruition in a Snake year, and Dragons have a sense of being in the right place at the right time. They could nurture key relationships.
- **Snake**
  Snakes stand a good chance of achieving their goals in their own year. New relationships show great potential, and established partnerships can flourish.
- **Horse**
  Mystery is disturbing to the straightforward Horse, so in a Snake year he or she must work hard to avoid unclear situations, especially in relationships.
- **Sheep**
  Sheep can enjoy a Snake year, taking chances confidently and reaping the rewards. This is also a good time for Sheep to make influential connections.
- **Monkey**
  Concealed issues at work and in relationships make situations unmanageable for Monkeys, who could rely on others to guide them through Snake energies.
- **Rooster**
  Roosters can make great personal and professional progress in a Snake year, especially in creative endeavours. This is a good year for relationship-building.
- **Dog**
  Last year was tough, but in this year Dogs are more at ease with events at home and at work. Dogs are advised to treat this as a period of consolidation.
- **Pig**
  Disharmony characterizes the Snake year for Pigs, who are advised to act conservatively and trust that any adverse effects should end with the year.

THE YEAR OF THE HORSE

HORSE YEARS: 2002 (WATER), 2014 (WOOD), 2026 (FIRE)
FIXED ELEMENT: FIRE   YANG SIGN

KEYWORDS
• CHANGE • FLEXIBILITY • SPEED • MOVEMENT • UNCERTAINTY
• ACTIVITY • IMPULSE • ACTION • VOLATILITY

GENERAL PROSPECTS

Fortunes can change fast in the year of the Horse, when ups and downs in luck, love and life are potentially the order of the day. In line with typical Horse characteristics, there's plenty of fast movement and very little standing still.
On the world stage this can mean that the global economy is particularly unstable in a Horse year, while the fortunes of any leading political party have to be closely monitored in order to give some sense of order. For individuals, personal and professional circumstances may change quickly, and the only sure way to deal with such uncertainty is to try to avoid impulsive action and show restraint. Such an environment can feel unsettling for the more timid and placid animals in the cycle, such as the Ox and the Sheep; while Dragons and Monkeys can thrive on the risky unpredictability of Horse energies.

The year of the Horse for the …

Rat
   Horse energy can push the Rat's love of risk that little bit further – but the result only emphasizes the year's volatility. Prudence will yield better results.

Ox
   Turbulence doesn't suit the steady Ox. However, perseverance and determination to stick with a sensible course carry Oxen through the chaos.

THE YEAR OF THE HORSE 馬

❀ Tiger
A Horse year is close to a Tiger's idea of heaven, bringing excellent financial, relationship and career prospects – as well as opportunities for travel.

❀ Rabbit
Both the Horse and the Rabbit are eager to connect with other people, so this is a good year for Rabbits to form relationships, including intimate ones.

❀ Dragon
The high jinks of a Horse year are no problem at all for the fiery Dragon, leading to plenty of activity, passion and potential for advancement.

❀ Snake
Snakes could try to be more straightforward in Horse years to avoid challenges from other individuals. Nurturing close relationships is key.

❀ Horse
A Horse's own year presents excellent opportunities to drive forward, discover adventure and reap rewards. Horses should follow their instincts.

❀ Sheep
Although there may be unwelcome drama this year, Horse energies also bring the Sheep positive potential for success – bringing goals within reach.

❀ Monkey
Monkeys can make the most of the Horse's speed and adventure, leading to self-advancement. But, they're also well advised not to get too carried away.

❀ Rooster
There's no plain sailing for Roosters this year – they're unsettled by volatile Horse energies. Roosters would do well to take care not to annoy others.

❀ Dog
This is a favourable and enjoyable year for the Dog, who's busy exploring new territories, taking opportunities, and generally having a good time.

❀ Pig
The year of the Horse is a period of hard work for the Pig, but it brings progress and enjoyment with it. Activities from earlier years now bear fruit.

PROSPECTS OVER TIME

THE YEAR OF THE SHEEP

SHEEP YEARS: 2003 (WATER), 2015 (WOOD), 2027 (FIRE)
FIXED ELEMENT: EARTH   YIN SIGN

KEYWORDS
• CALM • CONSIDERATION • SECURITY • STABILITY • PEACEFULNESS •
• CONTENTMENT • CONSOLIDATION • EASE • INERTIA •

GENERAL PROSPECTS

Following the active energy and the potential uncertainty of the preceding Horse year, the year of the Sheep ushers in a refreshing sense of peace. In keeping with Sheep characteristics, the year's energy creates more placid equilibrium. Healing and humane concerns may prevail – meaning that charitable bodies as well as the health and harmony of the family come to the fore. There's a greater sense of security in all things – whether at work, at home or in the world at large – and partnerships and relationships find a welcome ease. Sheep years are fruitful, in terms of the economy and personal endeavours, and there's an increased urge to care for the environment. A Sheep year is not the best time for radical new initiatives – rather, this is a year for consolidating what we already know and love, and for enjoying a reassuring sense of safety and stability.

The year of the Sheep for the …

Rat

This year Rats have good prospects at work, in relationships, and in financial affairs. The Rat may find an urge to express his or her creativity this year.

Ox

In this tricky year, Oxen may accept support from others to ensure their plans progress unhindered. Relationships will fare better than the Ox's career.

THE YEAR OF THE SHEEP 羊

- **Tiger**
  Tigers need one calm year in the 12-year cycle, and this is it. They could use this as a time for contemplation, allowing objectives to move along gently.
- **Rabbit**
  A sense of peace pervades this year for the Rabbit, giving good prospects for self-advancement in work and romance. Generally, this is a sociable year.
- **Dragon**
  To get the best out of a Sheep year, Dragons may simply complete projects that are underway, even if it feels frustrating not to be starting something new.
- **Snake**
  This is no time for radical change. Snakes should try for steady, quiet effort in line with Sheep energies, especially when it comes to making new contacts.
- **Horse**
  Horses need to think like Sheep for maximum benefits this year, making gentle progress, placing importance on relationships, and being shrewd and savvy.
- **Sheep**
  Sheep can use their own year to make changes that will best impact on their future. This is an excellent year for alliances and intimate relationships.
- **Monkey**
  This is a great year for Monkeys to pursue initiatives. They would do well to capitalize on some typical Sheep diplomacy to make valuable contacts.
- **Rooster**
  A Sheep year presents Roosters with the ideal opportunity for taking new steps in business and work. They must also make time for family and friends.
- **Dog**
  Challenges – especially at home – make it important for Dogs to build good relationships with family and friends this year. Positive changes can be made.
- **Pig**
  This is a satisfying year for the Pig, when past effort reaps rewards and memorable experiences are afoot. It's a happy time for romance and fun.

THE YEAR OF THE MONKEY

MONKEY YEARS: 2004 (WOOD), 2016 (FIRE), 2028 (EARTH)
FIXED ELEMENT: METAL   YANG SIGN

KEYWORDS
• UNPREDICTABILITY • TRANSITION • CHANGEABILITY • EXCITEMENT
• COMMUNICATION • INNOVATION • ENTERPRISE • UNCERTAINTY

GENERAL PROSPECTS

The year of the Monkey is characterized by unpredictability – just like the Monkey him- or herself. Events that happen this year are less likely to go according to plan, and dealings with other people may prove tricky. There may be deceit and deception lurking, too. However, if other signs can think and act like a Monkey – in other words, if they learn to be clever, nimble and flexible – they'll be able to adapt to changing circumstances and unexpected events without undue difficulty, and can emerge from the year unscathed. This is a favourable year for communication and enterprise – think innovation and collaboration. Last year was fairly static on the world stage, but this year finds momentum, with global economies gaining some ground (although not always favourably) and political plans springing into action.

The year of the Monkey for the …

❀ **Rat**
   This is a great year for the adventurous Rat, bringing inventiveness, high jinks and success. Personal relationships may turn tricky under Monkey influence.

❀ **Ox**
   Oxen dislike unpredictability, but taking one step at a time and holding steady in the face of chaos can enhance their reputations and advance their goals.

THE YEAR OF THE MONKEY 猴

❈ Tiger
Monkey energy undermines a Tiger's need for authority and respect, making this a difficult year. To ease relations, Tigers could avoid appearing arrogant.

❈ Rabbit
This is not a straightforward year for Rabbits, who are best using the time to gather perspectives rather than strive for results, particularly in business.

❈ Dragon
This is a fast and furious year for the Dragon, who should aim to keep up with the pace, learning to be adaptable and opportunistic, just like the Monkey.

❈ Snake
Snakes are advised to exercise caution during a Monkey year, taking nothing but romance at face value and looking for the subtext in events around them.

❈ Horse
Monkey influence promises the Horse a good year with many new alliances. Horses should capitalize on clever Monkey energy when aiming for their goals.

❈ Sheep
Sheep dislike unpredictability, but are advised to remember that not all surprises are unwelcome – focusing on being flexible can help smooth the way.

❈ Monkey
The Monkey's own year is a time for initiation, for relishing the excitement of new beginnings – and that includes the possibility of new relationships, too.

❈ Rooster
Existing relationships can get complicated for Roosters in a Monkey year, but professionally signs are good. They could prepare for bigger things next year.

❈ Dog
Professional and financial standing develops this year and Dogs can use the Monkey's energies to forge alliances. The Dog's social life will be good, too!

❈ Pig
Pigs are unnerved when things don't go to plan, but perseverance, patience, and using intelligence to manage change can help keep goals on track.

PROSPECTS OVER TIME

THE YEAR OF THE ROOSTER

ROOSTER YEARS: 2005 (WOOD), 2017 (FIRE), 2029 (EARTH)
FIXED ELEMENT: METAL   YIN SIGN

KEYWORDS
• CONFIDENCE • OPTIMISM • OUTSPOKENNESS • FLOURISH
• TREND-SETTING • CONFLICT • DETAIL • PICKINESS

GENERAL PROSPECTS

The year of the Rooster brings the possibility of positivity and optimism, giving all the animal signs better potential for a confident and progressive year. With Rooster energies filtering through, normally submissive or quiet signs such as the Sheep and the Rabbit may find their voices, speaking up for themselves though in other years they might not want to disturb the status quo. However, signs that are generally happy to express themselves vociferously are well advised to take care not to become too outspoken, as this could create an atmosphere that may lead to stand-offs or even conflict. There's definitely potential to make enemies in a Rooster year. Roosters are also finicky characters and in this year many people may be inclined to focus on too much detail. Finally, the year of the Rooster is an excellent time for fashion – check out the glorious designs on the catwalk.

The year of the Rooster for the …

❀ RAT

  This year Rats would do well to take a leaf out of the Rooster's book and deal with matters efficiently to capitalize on unlikely scenarios and tempt success.

❀ OX

  Oxen have found the last few years something of a challenge, but the Rooster brings fresh starts and forward progress – this is a good time for adventure.

THE YEAR OF THE ROOSTER 雞

- **Tiger**
  The Rooster's energy for self-promotion and financial success comes through for Tigers, but they must ensure new commitments are well thought through.
- **Rabbit**
  Rabbits should play it safe in a Rooster year. This isn't a time to make big changes, but with their ingenuity they can manage challenges as they come.
- **Dragon**
  Adventurous and courageous, Dragons have good possibility for success and advancement in a Rooster year. They may seize opportunities as they arise.
- **Snake**
  A Rooster year brings the Snake superb prospects in love and work. This is a year to build a good home life, and to find ways to make a mark on the world.
- **Horse**
  A Horse-like gallop is not suited to a Rooster year. To make progress, this is a time for Horses to be efficient and methodical, and to pay attention to detail.
- **Sheep**
  Sheep can enjoy personal advancement, new starts and relationship boosts in a Rooster year. They can harness the creative energy to set bold objectives.
- **Monkey**
  Monkeys are advised to learn from the Rooster's influence this year, becoming dedicated and consistent in their approach to tasks, and so reaping rewards.
- **Rooster**
  In their own year, Roosters enjoy excellent prospects for moving forward with objectives they already have in place, and find ultimate satisfaction at home.
- **Dog**
  The Rooster's busy schedule influences the Dog's calendar this year. Dogs need to stay positive to turn opportunities into real benefits at home or work.
- **Pig**
  Forward progress can be hard work in a Rooster year. Pigs should avoid risks, and work instead on developing their own knowledge, skills and well-being.

THE YEAR OF THE DOG

**DOG YEARS: 2006 (FIRE), 2018 (EARTH), 2030 (METAL)
FIXED ELEMENT: EARTH   YANG SIGN**

KEYWORDS
• CONSULTATIVE • CARING • NURTURING • ANXIOUS • UNEASY
• ALTRUISTIC • COMMITTED • FAMILIAL

GENERAL PROSPECTS

The year of the Dog brings with it concern for others. This is a year in which general welfare takes centre stage. Many of the signs in the cycle may experience the Dog's underlying altruistic energies and take on board the need to protect the well-being of people, animals, nature and the environment. Expect to feel a strong need to be around family and close friends – Dog years give a pervading sense of clannishness, which is reassuring for signs, such as the Rabbit and the Ox, who need anyway to be enveloped by those they love, but it can feel claustrophobic for those, such as the Tiger and the Horse, who normally like their freedom. Some signs may also feel a sense of unease or nervousness during a Dog year, and security (at home, personally and on the world stage) may become a prominent issue.

The year of the Dog for the …

❂ **Rat**

Dog energies give the Rat prospects for all-round good fortune. Rats are well advised to try not to overstretch themselves, accepting help when it's offered.

❂ **Ox**

Ox inflexibility can inhibit success in a Dog year, so Oxen need to temper their more bullish tendencies. An outgoing Ox could meet someone special.

THE YEAR OF THE DOG 狗

❈ **Tiger**

A Dog year is busy for Tigers, with good prospects on the home and romance fronts. They should accept offers of help and keep a cool head throughout.

❈ **Rabbit**

Love and work look good for the Rabbit in this year. With plenty of allies on hand for support, Rabbits might try to be a little more ambitious this year.

❈ **Dragon**

A Dog year is tricky for Dragons, so it's not a time for them to be innovative or outspoken. They'd do well to enjoy home life and prepare for next year.

❈ **Snake**

Snakes can be unusually active in this year. They'll gain good results if they complete projects they've started. Security matters may take precedence.

❈ **Horse**

Horses should capitalize on Dog influences by building new relationships and consolidating old ones – their own sense of adventure is the key to success.

❈ **Sheep**

In the Year of the Dog, Sheep are advised to take care to interact carefully with others, keeping communication friendly and avoiding stirring up controversy.

❈ **Monkey**

Monkeys appreciate the opportunities offered by Dog years, although they should take careful note of the details when they agree terms on any matter.

❈ **Rooster**

Roosters need to keep communication channels open, maintain standards and pay attention to detail to overcome the conflicting energies of a Dog year.

❈ **Dog**

The Dog's own year presents a positive shift after years of slow advancement. Dog-like tenacity pays off, with enhanced reputation and welcome progress.

❈ **Pig**

Pig and Dog energies are complementary, so a Dog year is a good time for a Pig to start long-term projects and relationships, and to help out with good causes.

PROSPECTS OVER TIME

THE YEAR OF THE PIG

PIG YEARS: 2007 (FIRE), 2019 (EARTH), 2031 (METAL)
FIXED ELEMENT: WATER   YIN SIGN

KEYWORDS
• STABILITY • HOME-MAKING • RELATIONSHIP-BUILDING
• HOUSEKEEPING • COMMUNITY • ORGANIZATION • COMPLETION

GENERAL PROSPECTS

The year of the Pig represents the last year in the 12-year cycle, and traditional Chinese astrology considers it the best period for sorting things out. This is a year to organize matters that have until now remained untended or have not been fully completed. In keeping with the characteristics of the Pig, expectations this year are for good fortune and positive energy. In addition, the economic and financial prospects for many of the signs generally look bright. The Pig is a sociable sign, so there can be a good community spirit pervading in this year, with plenty of new alliances on the horizon and the opportunity to cement budding friendships. On the world stage, nations may become more inward-looking during a Pig year, with fewer conflicts surfacing between countries and world politics generally settling down into relative equilibrium.

The year of the Pig for the …

Rat
Rats may find they need to work hard to make career progress this year, but the Pig's influence does make this a good time for Rats to improve alliances.

Ox
The Ox shares the Pig's love of the home, so this is a good year for Oxen to nurture their private lives. Pig energy helps Oxen make steady career progress.

THE YEAR OF THE PIG 豬

- **Tiger**
  During a Pig year, Tigers need to sort out any issues in their personal lives and try to use their Tiger-like zeal to ensure they seize opportunities for success.
- **Rabbit**
  Rabbits have the potential to really enjoy the year of the Pig with success, socializing and celebrating. There are especially good prospects for romance.
- **Dragon**
  In this year, the Dragon's life is on hold. He or she is best continuing to prepare for the future, perhaps seeing tangible benefits before the year is out.
- **Snake**
  Pig and Snake energies conflict, creating obstacles. A conservative attitude can maintain the status quo, while the Snake waits for things to improve.
- **Horse**
  Pig years are uneventful for the Horse, who makes no extreme gains or losses. However, a year off from frantic changes is a good way to rest and recharge.
- **Sheep**
  This is likely to be a very welcome, favourable year of progress for the Sheep, who makes gains in work, finance and relationships, and at home.
- **Monkey**
  Monkeys need to rein in their liking for trickery during a Pig year, with a more straightforward, cautious and patient approach producing the best results.
- **Rooster**
  Last year was pretty slow, but things are somewhat better all round for the Rooster in a Pig year. Good opportunities may come out of the blue.
- **Dog**
  A Pig year promises the Dog Pig-like feelings of enjoyment and satisfaction. Relationships with others are the key to progress in all areas of life.
- **Pig**
  In their own year, Pigs can reach some of their biggest goals, and enjoy the resulting adulation. There's a sense of things being in their rightful place.

CONCLUSIONS

The information in this book has enabled you to gain insight into your own personal nature and potential, your relationships with other people, and the changing patterns of your prospects over time. To conclude, I want to draw together some key lessons of Chinese astrology to highlight the ways in which you can gain the maximum benefit from everything you've learned.

- Each of us is subject to a complex combination of astrological influences. Chinese astrologers emphasize the crucial importance of looking at the whole picture rather than focusing on a few, particular aspects of your horoscope.
- Each sign possesses both positive and negative potential. No animal sign is inherently better than any other – every type can be happy or unhappy, fulfilled or unfulfilled, successful or unsuccessful; each one can make a valuable contribution to society. We should aim to make the most of our potential in life and relationships. This is how we create "good fortune".
- It's most accurate to regard astrological indications as tendencies and potential outcomes, rather than as cast-iron fate. Achieving good results in life depends on striving to fulfil the potential that astrology brings to your attention.
- Relationships are not only governed by astrological influences, they're very much what we make of them. Communication, compromise, commitment, trust and so on are always essential for making relationships stronger.
- When you look at your prospects over time, capitalize on the influences of each year, using the time wisely in relation to the energy of the prevailing animal. However, all types of year, even those that seem more difficult, can provide positive experiences from which we are able to grow and develop.

The information in this book is just the start of your journey into Chinese astrology. If you enjoyed it, please explore further!

INDEX

A
Affinity, Triangles of 154, 195
animal signs 30–31
 characteristics of 32–151
 hours of birth 21
 origins 15
 years of birth 25–7
ascendants 21, 22
astrology, Chinese 12–27, 220
 history 14–15
 individual interpretation 20–23
 relationships and 152–190
 year influences in 195

B
balance 23
birth hours 21
birth months 22
birth years 25–7

C
Chinese astrology 12–27, 220
 history 14–15
 individual interpretation 20–23
 in relationships 152–190
 and year influences 195
Chinese calendar 14, 22

Circle of Compatibility 154–5
Circle of Conflict 154–5, 195
compatibility 23, 153–5
 of individual signs 156–190
complementary signs 31, 195
Cycle of Control 18
cycle of influence 17, 20, 21
Cycle of Support 18

D
destiny 23–4
Dog 133–41
 health 141
 money 139
 preferences 140–41
 relationships 186–8
 work, career 138–9
 year influence 216–17
Dragon 73–81
 health 81
 money 79
 preferences 80
 relationships 168–70
 work, career 78–9
 year influence 204–5

E
Earth 16, 18

Earth Dog 137
Earth Dragon 77
Earth Horse 97
Earth Monkey 117
Earth Ox 47
Earth Pig 147
Earth Rabbit 67
Earth Rat 37
Earth Rooster 127
Earth Sheep 107
Earth Snake 87
Earth Tiger 57
Earth Fate 23
Elements 16–18, 31
 fixed 16, 17, 31
 mutable 17, 31
 year of birth 25–7

F
fate 23–4
Fire 16, 18
Fire Dog 136–7
Fire Dragon 76–7
Fire Horse 96–7
Fire Monkey 116–17
Fire Ox 46–7
Fire Pig 146–7
Fire Rabbit 66–7
Fire Rat 36–7
Fire Rooster 126–7
Fire Sheep 106–7
Fire Snake 86–7
Fire Tiger 56–7

INDEX

Five Elements 16–18, 31
  Cycle of Control 18
  Cycle of Support 18
  fixed 16, 17, 31
  mutable 17, 31
fixed Elements 16, 17, 31
fortune 24, 220
future prospects 192, 194–5
  for individual signs 196–219

G
good fortune 24, 220

H
happiness 24
harmony 23
Heaven Fate 23, 24
horoscopes
  creating 20–23
  history of 15
  interpreting 23–4, 30–31, 194–5
Horse 93–101
  health 101
  money 99
  preferences 100–101
  relationships 174–6
  work, career 98–9
  year influence 208–9
hours of birth 21
Human Fate 23–4

I
influence, cycle of 17, 20, 21
interpreting horoscopes 23–4, 30–31, 194–5

L
lunar calendar 14, 22
lunar months 22

M
Metal 16, 18
  Metal Dog 134
  Metal Dragon 74
  Metal Horse 94
  Metal Monkey 114
  Metal Ox 44
  Metal Pig 144
  Metal Rabbit 64
  Metal Rat 34
  Metal Rooster 124
  Metal Sheep 104
  Metal Snake 84
  Metal Tiger 54
Monkey 113–21
  health 121
  money 119
  preferences 120–21
  relationships 180–82
  work, career 118
  year influence 212–13
month of birth 22
mutable Elements 17, 31

O
opposite signs 31, 155, 195
Ox 43–51
  health 51
  money 49
  preferences 50
  relationships 159–61

  work, career 48–9
  year influence 198–9

P
Pig 143–51
  health 151
  money 149
  preferences 150–51
  relationships 189–90
  work, career 148–9
  year influence 218–19
prospects over time 192, 194–5
  for individual signs 196–219

R
Rabbit 63–71
  health 71
  money 69
  preferences 70
  relationships 165–7
  work, career 68–9
  year influence 202–3
Rat 33–41
  health 41
  money 39
  preferences 40–41
  relationships 156–8
  work, career 38
  year influence 196–7
relationships 152, 153–5
  for the Dog 186–8
  for the Dragon 168–70
  for the Horse 174–6
  for the Monkey 180–82
  for the Ox 159–61
  for the Pig 189–90

INDEX

for the Rabbit 165–7
for the Rat 156–8
for the Rooster 183–5
for the Sheep 177–9
for the Snake 171–3
for the Tiger 162–4
lunar month influence 22
support and control cycles 18
yin and yang 19
rising sign 21, 22
Rooster 123–31
health 131
money 129
preferences 130
relationships 183–5
work, career 128–9
year influence 214–15

S
60-year cycle 17, 20, 21
Self Fate 23, 24
Sheep 103–11
health 111
money 109
preferences 110–11
relationships 177–9
work, career 108–9
year influence 210–11
Snake 83–91
health 91
money 89
preferences 90
relationships 171–3
work, career 88
year influence 206–7
Support Cycle 18

T
Tiger 53–61
health 61
money 59
preferences 60–61
relationships 162–4
work, career 58–9
year influence 200–201
Triangles of Affinity 154, 195

W
Water 16, 18
Water Dog 135
Water Dragon 75
Water Horse 95
Water Monkey 115
Water Ox 44–5
Water Pig 145
Water Rabbit 64–5
Water Rat 34–5
Water Rooster 125
Water Sheep 105
Water Snake 85
Water Tiger 54–5
Wood 16, 18
Wood Dog 135–6
Wood Dragon 75–6
Wood Horse 95–6
Wood Monkey 115–16
Wood Ox 45–6
Wood Pig 145–6
Wood Rabbit 65–6
Wood Rat 35–6
Wood Rooster 125–6
Wood Sheep 105–6
Wood Snake 85–6
Wood Tiger 55–6

Y
year influences 192, 194–5
of the Dog 216–17
of the Dragon 204–5
of the Horse 208–9
of the Monkey 212–13
of the Ox 198–9
of the Pig 218–19
of the Rabbit 202–3
of the Rat 196–7
of the Rooster 214–15
of the Sheep 210–11
of the Snake 206–7
of the Tiger 200–201
year of birth chart 25–7
yin and yang 17, 19

AUTHOR'S ACKNOWLEDGMENTS

I would like to express deep appreciation to the following people for their support in producing this book: My literary agent and great friend, Susan Mears; consultant Shuen-Lian Hsaio; creative staff at Watkins Publishing including Michael Mann, Bob Saxton, Judy Barratt, Roger Walton, Suzanne Tuhrim, Josephine Bonde, Harvey Chan and Tristan Tan – it was a pleasure to work with you all on this project; … and all the teachers who have informed me on the subjects of Chinese astrology and Oriental philosophy over the last three decades.

If you would like any further information about Gerry or his work, please contact him on www.gerrymaguirethompson.com.